T0301617

Taxation and the Promotion of Human Happiness

Taxation and the Promotion of Human Happiness

An Essay by George Warde Norman

Edited by
D.P. O'Brien

Emeritus Professor of Economics
University of Durham, UK

with

John Creedy

The Truby Williams Professor of Economics
University of Melbourne, Australia

Edward Elgar
Cheltenham, UK • Northampton, MA, USA

Published by
Edward Elgar Publishing Limited
The Lypiatts
15 Lansdown Road
Cheltenham
Glos GL50 2JA
UK

Edward Elgar Publishing, Inc.
William Pratt House
9 Dewey Court
Northampton
Massachusetts 01060
USA

A catalogue record for this book
is available from the British Library

Library of Congress Control Number: 2009921839

ISBN 978 1 84844 485 0

Printed and bound in Great Britain by MPG Books Ltd, Bodmin, Cornwall

Contents

Acknowledgements   ix
Preface   xi
Introduction   xv
Bibliography   xli

Essay on Taxation

I Introduction

1 Political Economy and Taxation   1

2 Advantages of Taxation   7

II Qualities of Taxation

3 Taxes and Other Sources of Revenue   15

4 Computability   21

5 Simplicity   27

6 Frugality in Collection   31

7 Constancy   37

8 Divisibility   39

9 Popularity   41

10 Noninterference   45

11 Equality   53

12 Uncorruptiveness   59

13 Unvexatiousness   65

14 Unevasibility   69

III   Review of Existing or Supposed Taxes

15 Motive Influencing the Framers of Taxes   75

16 General Observations on Indirect Taxes   83

17 Custom House Duties   93

18 The Excise Monopolies   101

19 Taxes on Particular Classes or Persons   109

20 Direct Taxes on Objects of Luxury   113

21 Taxes on Travelling and the Conveyance of Intelligence   117

22 Taxes on Justice   123

23 Taxes on the Transfer of Property, on Knowledge, on
   Prudence, on Ingenuity, and on Health   129

24 Taxes on Rent, Tythe, Land Tax   135

25 Continuation of Taxes on Rent, Poor Rate, House and
   Window Tax   143

26 The Poll-Tax   151

27 Legacy Duty and Stamp Duty on Probates of Wills   155

28 The Assessed Taxes and Stamp Duties   159

29 Turnpike and Bridge Tolls, Barrières and Harbour and
   Light Dues   163

Contents

30 Taxes on Vices   **167**

31 The Income Tax in England   **171**

32 An Improved Property Tax   **177**

33 Proposals for Reform   **185**

Index   **199**

Acknowledgements

In the preparation of this edition, by far the biggest debt is owed to John Creedy. Knowing of the existence of Norman's manuscript *Essay on Taxation*, and of earlier work that I had done on it, he encouraged me to return to it, overcoming my hesitations, and to provide the editorial material suitable for a modern edition.

But this was only the start. Employing both editorial and technical skills to a remarkable degree, he structured the presentation of Norman's *Essay* in such a way that it is now perfectly approachable by a modern reader. He then produced the completed text, incorporating my editorial material. My debt for all this cannot be overstated, and without John's input, at every stage, the edition itself would never have appeared.

I must also thank the Norman family, in the person of Canon W.B. Norman, the head of the Kent branch of the Norman family, for renewing the permission originally given by his father, the late General C.W. Norman, to publish the *Essay*. The resources of the Durham University Library, and above all of its Document Delivery (Inter-Library Loan) Service have also proved very valuable in the preparation of the editorial notes. I must also thank the 1960s staff of Kent County Archives who co-operated most helpfully with my work on the Norman papers, in connection with my preparation of *The Correspondence of Lord Overstone*, and who in particular provided me with Xerox copies of the mass of manuscript which constituted the various versions and revisions of Norman's *Essay*.

Preface

In the late 1960s, when I was working on the papers of Samuel Jones Loyd, Lord Overstone, Norman's close friend and collaborator in the struggles around the development of a regime of monetary control in Britain,[1] I visited the late General C.W. Norman at his home at West Farleigh, near Maidstone. There, on a shelf in the library, I spotted a volume which did not appear to be a normal book. My curiosity aroused, I examined it and discovered that it was Norman's *Autobiography*, of the existence of which I had no idea. Nor, it seemed, had General and Mrs Norman. They were as surprised as I was at the discovery.

I was taken to the Kent County Record Office at Maidstone by General Norman, and introduced to the Archivist, Dr Felix Hull. I was given access to the Norman papers, and amongst those, under one general heading of U310, F37 'Manuscripts of essays and speeches probably written by George Warde Norman', there proved to be no less than four boxes of material relating to Norman. They included, in particular, copies of unpublished essays and a major work – the *Essay on Taxation*.

Norman, despite limited education provided by Eton, had great intellectual curiosity and energy, and put pen to paper on a wide variety of subjects from archaeology and geology to the theory of international trade (he provided a penetrating critique of the famous Cuba Case put forward by the

---

[1]D.P. O'Brien (ed.) (1971) *The Correspondence of Lord Overstone* (3 volumes). Cambridge: Cambridge University Press.

Irish economist Robert Torrens) and the theory of monetary control. But he was an individual of acute nervousness, and this nervousness made him extremely reluctant to allow his writings to see the light of day. The *Essay on Taxation* was never published, though a later work, on the pressure of taxation and the role of government expenditure, was published in 1850.[2]

Yet Norman was extremely attached to the *Essay on Taxation*, as the manuscripts in Kent County Record Office at Maidstone make very clear. Though he began the work late in 1821, as his *Autobiography* relates, he returned to it again and again over the years, inserting paragraphs, deleting others, and eventually commissioning an amanuensis, Robert Turner, to produce a fair copy of the whole thing. Possibly at that stage he had in mind publication. Yet, once again, he was not satisfied. The manuscript in Maidstone on which Robert Turner laboured – and this must have been no small task, given Norman's handwriting – contains numerous additions, amendments, deletions and insertions subsequent to the fair copy, in Norman's hand. At one stage Norman even prepared an abridged version for publication in a journal. A copy of this version is still amongst his papers in Maidstone. Yet in the end the *Essay* was never published.

In preparing the present edition, Norman's chapter structure has been retained, though chapter numbering has been made continuous in the modern style, rather than following Norman in employing a new sequence of chapter numbers for each section of the *Essay*. This aids cross reference.

For the most part, the text follows a copy which was prepared in the late 1960s in Belfast, using Turner's manuscript but incorporating the extra paragraphs which Norman wrote in the margins of Turner's foolscap sheets, and also employing Norman's own manuscript for the clarification of points and for the addition of two amplificatory paragraphs which, though not deleted, did not make the journey from Norman's original to Turner's fair copy.

---

[2]G.W. Norman (1850) *An Examination of Some Prevailing Opinions, as to the Pressure of Taxation in This, and Other Countries*. 4th edition. London: T.&W. Boone (1864).

The 1960s typescript was scanned, cleaned up and put into a format of a kind acceptable to the modern reader. Norman's strange punctuation practices, no doubt the product of his Eton education, have necessitated some adjustment in the interests of comprehension of the text, though the end result is faithful to Norman's work. Editorial notes have been placed within square brackets.

Norman's *Autobiography* is of such interest both in its own right, and in illuminating the context of the *Essay*, that separate publication of an edited edition is in preparation. Taken together, these two documents should help to provide not only an appreciation of an individual who, for all his retiring nature, was an important influence on the development of monetary control in Britain, one who was a committed Utilitarian, a close friend of George Grote (until their quarrel) and of Charles Hey Cameron, both of them prominent Utilitarian thinkers. The *Autobiography* and the *Essay on Taxation* thus provide an insight into the Utilitarian background in the early and mid nineteenth century.

D.P. O'Brien

Introduction

'Towards the end of 1821, I commenced an Essay on Taxation, redolent of Bentham and Mill – the object being to shew, how the Revenue of a Country might be levied with least pressure on the Taxpayers – The conclusion to which I came was that a single Property Tax and that only was the scheme which offered the greatest advantages, as taking least from individuals and imposing the fewest sacrifices on them – I was so far I believe right. If people could only be found to agree with me in feeling – but that they never will do, and it is probable that an attempt to establish one sole Tax in England, or France, would infallibly fail, and if persisted in, occasion commotions and civil war – ...My Essay on Taxation was never printed but still exists in MS – It cost me a vast deal of thought and labour – I may here remark that I have ever found Composition to involve a severe strain on my whole Organism – one reason why I have written comparatively so little – Perhaps if I had tried narrative or description, instead of subjects involving so much of argumentation, I should have been able to write more and better.' G.W. Norman *Autobiography*.

The Utilitarian Background

Norman's *Essay* is an extremely interesting document, both in relation to its contents and to the environment in which it was produced. Taxation was a matter of continuing concern to Norman. As we shall see, he later produced a work on the pressure of taxation and the appropriates size of government expenditure (Norman, 1850) which led to controversy with the Irish economist John Elliot Cairnes, who occupied the chair of Political Economy at University College London.[3]

---

[3]Material relating to the dispute with Cairnes over the weight of taxation will be found in O'Brien (1971, Vol. III, pp. 1049-1050, 1502-1506).

His interest, as manifested in the *Essay*, is combined with a thoroughgoing Utilitarian approach. Indeed it is fascinating to see the influence exerted by Utilitarianism on a young, highly intelligent, and largely self-educated member of the upper classes. Norman was not perhaps completely representative; through his connection with George Grote, the historian of Greece, whose own background was also in the financial sector, the influence of Utilitarianism was no doubt stronger on him than on many of his contemporaries.[4]

Yet others were undoubtedly borne along by this intellectual tide; the outstanding figures of Bentham, James Mill, and John Stuart Mill were simply the leaders of an extremely influential body of individuals. What Norman set out was a Utilitarian guide to taxation, even though, ironically, the proposals are not as Bentham himself would have formulated them. Thus Norman did not make use of Bentham's severe criterion that any proposed expenditure should be compared with the hurt done by 'an equal portion of the produce of the most vexatious and burthensome tax' (Bentham, 1843, Vol. II, p. 202); he had nothing to say about Bentham's various schemes to provide finance for government; and he certainly did not agree, as will be clear from the *Essay*, that indirect taxes were 'relatively the least obnoxious because they can be collected with less vexation to the taxpayer than direct ones' (Stark, 1952, Vol. III, p. 45). This in itself is an interesting indication of the way that Utilitarianism, while providing inspiration and a secular standard of right and wrong in public policy, was very far from being a cut and dried body of doctrine. The younger Utilitarians moved away from the Master's precise proposals while continuing to adhere to the standard of the greatest happiness of the greatest number as their test of right and wrong.

In his *Essay*, Norman formulates a sort of legislator's guide; a set of criteria which should be used in achieving the Utilitarian goal. It should be used

---

[4]As Bentham's modern editor has written: 'Without Dumont, without John Stuart Mill, without George Grote and a few others we would know very little of Bentham's thought' (Stark, 1952, Vol. I, p. 11).

in evaluating existing taxation, and it should act as a guide to those imposing taxes. Thus the criteria are set out in terms of the maximisation of human happiness in the aggregate. This is highly significant because although, as we shall see, Norman's set of criteria had more in common with Adam Smith's four canons of taxation than, perhaps, he was prepared to admit even to himself, the focus was not, as it had been for Smith, economic growth. Instead for Norman it was the maximisation of human happiness, in a way which was essentially static in its approach. This is in significant contrast to McCulloch, the most important Classical writer on taxation after Smith; for McCulloch evaluated fiscal policy very largely in terms of its actual or potential impact on economic growth. Norman, in contrast, focused on what he believed to be the scientific achievement of Benthamism in formulating the guiding principle of the greatest happiness of the greatest number.

The Canons of Taxation: Adam Smith

In order to set Norman's discussion in context, it is appropriate to compare it with Adam Smith's four canons of taxation. They are:

1. **Equality.** 'The subjects of every state ought to contribute towards the support of the government, as nearly as possible, in proportion to their respective abilities; that is, in proportion to the revenue which they respectively enjoy under the protection of the state.'

2. **Certainty.** 'The tax which each individual is bound to pay ought to be certain, and not arbitrary. The time of payment, the manner of payment, the quantity to be paid, ought all to be clear and plain to the contributor, and to every other person.'

3. **Convenience of Payment**. 'Every tax ought to be levied at the time, or in the manner, in which it is most likely to be convenient for the contributor to pay it.'

4. **Economy in Collection**. 'Every tax ought to be so contrived as both to take out and to keep out of the pockets of the people as little as possible, over and above what it brings in to the public treasury of the state' (Smith, 1776, pp. 350-351).

Norman's Maxims of Taxation

Norman initially approached the subject of an optimal tax system by way of stating four maxims of taxation. They are:

1. Minimising the number of public employees;

2. Paying only the minimum supply price for public employees;

3. Substituting honours for pecuniary rewards;

4. 'Levying the sum, which after the application of the above rules, may still be required for the use of the state in such a way as may occasion the smallest possible diminution of the general happiness'.

It is on this last maxim that all of Norman's attention is concentrated. While the first three maxims suggest minimisation of public expenditure for a given programme of state activity, Norman's entire focus is on the revenue side of the account. There is no consideration of benefit. The approach is entirely an ability-to-pay one. There is no consideration, apart from generalised statements about the civilising effects of taxation and government, of a balancing of tax and benefit. The needs of the state are taken as given, and the entire focus is on ability to pay. Smith's first canon had combined both ability to pay and benefit; Norman simply took the needs of the state as given.

Focusing on ability to pay itself was designed to lead to a system in which payment of taxes led to an equal proportional sacrifice of utility; this, Norman believed, should leave taxpayers in the same relative position as before tax. Like J.S. Mill he assumed that this would produce least aggregate sacrifice. As we shall see, that is not in fact the case.

In adopting an ability to pay approach, Norman was certainly in the mainstream of nineteenth century Classical writers on taxation. Nevertheless, and despite Norman's strictures against excessive remuneration of public employees, such an approach can lead to a situation in which the role of the state can be expanded without apparent limit, and without considering whether such an expansion conforms with any Utilitarian ideals. This is especially the case for someone like Norman who, as is apparent from the early part of this *Essay* where he considers taxation as a mark of civilisation and from his 1850 essay cited above, was actually supportive of an increasing role for government.

Criteria for Minimum Sacrifice

In order to meet the aim of minimising the loss of human happiness, in raising a given revenue, Norman attempts to find a set of criteria by which the goodness of a tax can be judged. He struggled with this. In a letter to George Grote he posited the concept of 'moral equality' – a tax was 'morally prodigal' if it imposed a loss of welfare through an inquisitorial nature, and it was 'morally unequal' if it imposed unequal sacrifices on different classes. Under the heading of 'frugality' he included not only the question of the expenses of collection but also compliance costs imposed on the taxpayer. He struggled to find a nomenclature, and at one stage was contemplating words like 'viceincentiveness' and, correspondingly, 'viceincentive' to indicate the social harm which might be done by a tax.[5]

But it rather looks as if the classification of qualities on which Norman

---

[5]The manuscript is in the Norman papers. It is reproduced in O'Brien (1971, Vol. I, pp. 188-189).

finally settled owed a good deal to Overstone. For in a document amongst Norman's papers, offered as a criticism of the *Essay*, we find Overstone suggesting that a tax should have the following qualities: it should be productive, computable, divisible, frugal, non-interferent, unannoyant, equal, popular, and uncorruptive. This corresponds very well with Norman's final classification though, given his concern with the effects of customs duties, he also attached importance to 'unevasibility'. Though Norman's classification of desirable characteristics is wider, as comparison with the tables below show, the core of it is Overstone's.[6] Norman's final classification involved the following requirements of a tax. Taxes must be *frugal* (this is simply Smith's fourth canon), *computable* (the anticipated revenues should be calculable), *simple*, *constant* (in their yield at given tax rates), and *divisible*. By this last Norman meant that they should be flexible in the rates levied, in order to meet varying annual revenue requirements of the state.

A tax should also be *popular*, Norman believed. This was however only a relatively minor matter as far as he was concerned; on several occasions in the *Essay*, Norman argues that if a tax is a good tax according to his other criteria, but not popular, the government should try to persuade people to overcome their aversion towards it. Moreover, it becomes evident at the end of the *Essay* that Norman's opinion of democratic views on taxation was not high. Essentially he seems to have believed that whether or not a tax is a good tax or not was independent of its popularity, though a requirement of popularity, however misguided public understanding might be in Norman's opinion, constrained government.

A tax should also be *'non-interferent'*. What Norman meant here was that a tax should not interfere with the allocation of resources. He had entirely digested Smith's message concerning the optimal allocation of resources through the pursuit of enlightened self-interest, though without perhaps see-

---

[6]The document is reproduced in O'Brien (1971, Vol. I, pp. 198-200).

ing this clearly, as Smith had done, in the context of economic growth. That was to be the topic of his later excursion into tax literature (Norman, 1850).

A tax should be *equal*. Smith had placed equality at the head of his canons of taxation. As already noted, Smith had managed in his statement of the requirement of equality to conflate both equality with respect to the resources of the taxpayer (ability to pay) and equality with respect to the benefits enjoyed by the taxpayer under the state (the benefit principle), quite possibly assuming that the two necessarily, or at least normally, coincided. Norman, like many of his contemporaries, confined himself to the first of these, ability to pay. His conclusion was that equality required proportionality. A tax should be proportional to the resources of the taxpayer. This was because, according to Norman's understanding of least aggregate sacrifice of welfare, a tax should leave taxpayers in the same relative position after tax as before tax.

Norman had clearly given a good deal of thought to this question, and in particular to the possibility that progression might reduce aggregate sacrifice to a minimum. Of course this raises the question of precisely what degree of progression, up to outright confiscation, would be dictated by the Utilitarian requirement. In the end Norman was forced to accept McCulloch's view that proportionality was the only rule that could be followed. As McCulloch had put it forcefully, once proportionality was departed from, those responsible for setting tax rates were at sea without rudder or compass (1845, p. 147).

Like J.S. Mill many years later (Mill, 1848, Book V, Chapter II), Norman seems to have been satisfied that equal proportional sacrifice of utility would in any case be achieved by proportional taxation. Subsequent writers, notably Cohen-Stuart (1958, pp. 48-71), have shown that this is not necessarily the case. Moreover, as Edgeworth and Pigou later pointed out, least aggregate sacrifice involved equal marginal sacrifice, which could in principle, with known and identical utility schedules, involve levelling of incomes down from the top, an outcome which Norman certainly would not have favoured. But even the idea of equal proportional sacrifice of utility turns out to imply the need for different tax regimes, proportional, progressive, or even regressive, depending on the relative rates of decline of average and marginal utility of income (O'Brien, 2004, p. 303).

Norman's support for proportionality was buttressed with arguments provided by George Grote, himself an important Utilitarian influence on Norman, as already noted. Although Grote's understanding of economics in general was poor,[7] he provided an important Utilitarian perspective on the early drafts of Norman's *Essay*.

In a general comment on the work, Grote professed himself very happy with Norman's *Essay*, but he was fundamentally critical of the treatment of equality.[8] This was because, in his original version of the *Essay*, Norman had justified equality not on utilitarian principles but on a vague appeal to human instinct. Grote however insisted that it must be justified on utilitarian grounds, as the *Essay* was itself grounded on utilitarianism. He wrote to Norman: 'Equality of taxation is a particular case of the principle of utility, just in the same manner as the respect of property, & general observance of other branches of justice, is.'

Accordingly, Grote's justification of proportionality in taxation proceeded as follows. Firstly, 'equality of privation' – of welfare loss – requires exemption from taxation of a subsistence minimum of income or property. To tax

---

[7]This is clear from a document about value theory which, with great confidence it would seem, to judge from the tone, Grote sent to Norman. His argument concerning variations in profit rates and wages – he contended that they did not affect relative values but affected all commodities equally – can only be understood on the basis of assuming uniform capital/labour coefficients across all industries. It would appear that Grote was unaware of the implications of Ricardo's famous section IV of the chapter on value in the third edition of the latter's *Principles* (Ricardo, 1821, pp. 30-38), which substantially (indeed more substantially than Ricardo realised – O'Brien, 2004, pp. 98-101) modified his labour theory of value. His assertion that the employment of capital was secondary to, and dependent on, that of labour proceeds on the implicit assumption of fixed capital/labour ratios within industries. Grote's document is reproduced in O'Brien (1971, Vol. I, pp. 190-195). The original is in the Norman papers.

[8]Grote's general criticism is reproduced in O'Brien (1971, pp. 195-198). The original is in the Norman papers.

that would take away from somebody 'his life ... his whole powers of enjoyment altogether'. The next question was the appropriate scale for taxation, beyond the subsistence minimum. Grote believed, like John Stuart Mill later (1848, pp. 804-805), that the poor gained more from good government than the rich. In the absence of good government, the rich were not only able to protect themselves but were also able to oppress the poor. This in itself implied a case for a regressive tax regime. But regression in turn left the middle classes, whom Grote implicitly equated with those setting the tax rates, to make up for the shortfall of revenue because those above them in the income scale were contributing less than in proportion to their means. This ruled out regressive tax scales, for practical purposes. Progression, on the other hand, introduced a vulnerability argument. Like McCulloch (1845, pp. 146-147), Grote argued that if one class taxed those above it more than in proportion to tax-paying resources, the taxing class might itself be attacked, in time, from below.[9] Thus the utilitarian argument arrived at proportionality as the expression of equality in taxation. Grote believed that proportionality would maximise (post tax) welfare, thus implicitly accepting that it involved least aggregate sacrifice. This is particularly arbitrary since he explicitly posited non-uniform welfare functions.

Nonetheless, Norman's scheme, like that of his contemporaries amongst the Classical economists, actually involved a degree of progression (Mill, 1848, pp. 606-7; O'Brien, 2004, p. 302) because there was a 'subsistence minimum' exempted from taxation in his proposals.

Norman also believed that taxes should be *'uncorruptive'*. Customs duties – these were Norman's particular hatred, partly due to his experiences as a

---

[9]The commonality of this argument with McCulloch, who certainly was not a Utilitarian, suggests that concern over prospective widening of the franchise lay behind Grote's concern on that score, despite his political activity as a radical. In a generation that was to see the turmoil leading to the great Reform Act of 1832, it was understandable, indeed, that progression had the potential to be used as a weapon to subvert security of property – even the entire economic arrangements of society.

timber importer and partly due to his childhood experiences of the Sussex town of Hastings – corrupted whole towns, he reported. The smugglers in Hastings were regarded with approbation by the townsfolk.

Taxes should also be *'unvexatious'* and *'unevasible'*. The former echoes Smith's third requirement – Convenience. The latter was to prove a particularly sensitive point, given Norman's advocacy of income and property taxation, and the history of the operation of the British income tax up to 1816, when, being very unpopular, it was abolished. One of the main reasons for its unpopularity was public awareness that it was, as McCulloch indeed pointed out, a tax upon honesty in the making of a tax return (1845, p. 120). Evasion, which was in practice extremely easy, prospered, and honesty was penalised.

Direct versus Indirect Taxation

Norman was extremely unusual among his contemporaries in his strong preference for direct taxation.[10] Indeed he is dismissive of those who opposed direct taxation. At the start of chapter 27 he refers to 'that dislike which prevails to an absurd and irrational extent in the public mind against all direct taxes whatever, and which also makes them to be considered vexatious'. There were a number of other advocates of direct taxation (O'Brien, 1999), but enthusiastic support for it was really only to be found amongst writers outside the mainstream, who attracted little general support.

Tax Incidence

Norman's analysis of tax incidence was a marriage of Benthamism and standard Classical analysis. His starting point is that taxation policy should aim at inflicting least aggregate sacrifice. But what was critical was not the

---

[10]See O'Brien (2004, pp. 294-295) on attitudes amongst the Classical economists to this choice.

absolute amount of sacrifice of welfare, but the ratio of that sacrifice to the revenue resulting from the tax causing the welfare loss. A tax which was highly productive of revenue but which caused a large welfare loss could still be preferred to one that caused a smaller absolute welfare loss.

The welfare loss itself had two parts. Firstly there was what Norman called the 'economical effect', which was the taxpayer's loss of command over resources consequent upon the tax. Secondly there was what he called the 'moral' effects of taxation. Prominent among these were the incentives to crime, the upsetting effect produced by taxation, and disruption of the normal channels of economic activity. Raising taxes to a level which passed their revenue-maximisation point intensified these negative moral effects. Unpopularity also increased the welfare loss resulting from a tax.

The moral effects were also, at least to some extent, in the nature of deadweight losses. Norman also identified a more conventional kind of deadweight loss, in particular in relation to protective duties. His analysis is interesting and, despite a slip in his presentation,[11] it is worth looking at a bit more carefully. In chapter 10 he identifies, by means of a numerical example, both the conventional deadweight loss and also a resource misallocation loss.

Norman's analysis can be explained by the use of Figure 1, showing the British demand for silk, where P(F) is the price of French silk, P(UK) is the price of British silk produced domestically, and P(F)+T is the price of French silk in Britain after the introduction of a tariff. Consumers initially demand OQ_1 of silk, which is all satisfied by imports of French silk. A tariff of T per unit of silk is imposed to protect British producers. If silk produced in both countries were considered by consumers to be of a similar quality, they would purchase, after the tariff, no French silk and consume OQ_3, all made up of British silk. But consumers are prepared to import from France the first OQ_2 units at the higher price because of the higher quality. Hence the tariff

---

[11]Norman referred to a proportional rather than an absolute change in price.

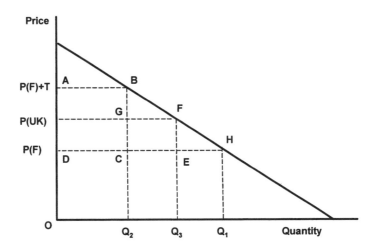

Figure 1: Norman's Analysis of Tariffs

revenue is given by the area ABCD. A quantity $OQ_3 - OQ_2$ of the inferior British silk is consumed, so the area CEFG measures resource misallocation. Hence the area EFH is a measure of the conventional deadweight loss.

The presence of material borrowed from standard Classical analysis provides an interesting indication of the extent to which Norman was part of the 'scientific community' of the Classical economists. Thus he argued that taxes on 'monopolised' articles (he meant cases of less than perfect elasticity of supply) fall on the producer. He was following Nassau Senior here in his understanding of 'monopoly' (O'Brien, 2004, p. 118). In fact they do so only partially, as any first year economics student could demonstrate. Taxes on competitively produced items fall, Norman argued, on the consumer. This was, again, a standard Classical position. The underlying assumption was perfect elasticity of supply. Taxes on 'wage goods' – that is to say, on part of the minimal consumption budget of the labouring classes – are passed on, and reduce profits. The argument is the standard Classical one that, with wages at subsistence, there is no scope for reducing real wages any further, and so wages must rise, and profits, especially in a Ricardian world, be reduced. As a position it is extremely unsatisfactory (O'Brien, 2004, pp. 296-297), and Norman was forced to recognise that such a transfer of the tax burden could be a very long drawn out process, resulting in significant hardship in the interim.

Norman also held that taxes on particular occupations, or particular individuals, would simply result in alterations in relative prices. This again was standard Classical analysis, resting on the proposition that post-tax net rate of return had to be equalised between different employments of capital. Taxes on rent he believed to be those on an intra-marginal surplus, a standard Ricardian argument which was subject to a host of qualifications in other writers (O'Brien, 2004, pp. 299-300). Norman also attempted to analyse the incidence of taxes on houses, and the poor rate, although it was not until Edgeworth that the incidence of such taxes was satisfactorily resolved (O'Brien, 1970, pp. 252-253).

Taxes Evaluated

Having established his intellectual framework, Norman then proceeded to examine existing taxes in the light of his requirement of a good tax system. Tables 1 and 2 summarise his findings.

Before proceeding to the detailed discussion of actual and potential taxes, Norman begins Part III of the *Essay* with some guiding principles in addition to the maxims already discussed. These are, firstly, that government expenditure should be minimised (a position he was to abandon in his 1850 work). Secondly, taxation should only be imposed for revenue purposes, and not for such purposes as sumptuary taxes or protective duties, to alter the natural allocation of resources, to favour social groups, or for national defence. Only by observing these constraints would the Utilitarian objective of minimising the welfare loss, which was inescapable when taxes were levied,

Table 1: Norman's Classification of Taxes by their Qualities: Part A

	Compu-table	Simple	Frugal	Constant	Divi-sible	Popular
Customs	no	no				yes
Excise	no			no	no	yes
Partial taxes	no			no	no	
Luxuries	yes	no	no	no	no	yes
Travelling	no	yes		no	no	yes
Justice	no	yes	yes	no	no	
Property transfer	no	yes	yes	no	no	yes
Knowledge	no	yes	yes	no	no	yes
Insurance	no	yes	yes	no	no	yes
Ingenuity	no	yes	yes	no	no	yes
Health	no	yes	yes	no	no	yes
Tithe	no		no	no	no	no
Modus	yes	yes		yes	yes	yes
Poor rate	yes	yes	yes	yes	yes	
Window tax						
Poll tax	yes	yes	no	yes	yes	
Legacy probate	no		yes	no	no	no
Assessed stamps			yes		yes	no
Transport		yes	yes			yes
Vice	no	yes		no	no	yes
Income tax	yes	yes	yes		yes	no
Single property tax	yes		yes	yes	yes	

Table 2: Norman's Classification of Taxes by their Qualities: Part B

	Non-interferent	Equal	Uncor-ruptive	Unvex-atious	Unevas-ive	Chpt
Customs	no	no	no	no	no	16, 17
Excise	no	no	no	no	no	16, 18
Partial taxes	no					19
Luxuries	yes	no	yes	no		20
Travelling	no	no	no	yes		21
Justice	no	no	no			22
Property transfer	no		no	yes	yes	23
Knowledge	no		no	yes	yes	23
Insurance	no		no	yes	yes	23
Ingenuity	no		no	yes	yes	23
Health	no		no	yes	yes	22
Tithe	no		yes		yes	24
Modus			yes			24
Poor rate	yes	no	yes		yes	25
Window tax			no			25
Poll Tax	yes			no	yes	26
Legacy probate	yes	no			yes	27
Assessed stamps	no					28
Transport		no	no			29
Vice	yes	no	no	yes	no	30
Income tax	yes	no	no			31
Single property tax	yes					32

be achieved.[12]

But there was an important rider, and it was one which helps to explain how, later in the *Essay*, Norman was able to ride roughshod over most of the objections to his favoured income and, especially, property taxes. This was the point he had made much earlier, in chapter 4, and referred to on subsequent occasions. The harm done by any taxes must be balanced against the revenue which they were capable of raising; quite serious harm might be tolerable if the revenue raising capacity of a tax were more than proportionately large.

This was not however the case with the harm which Norman attributed to many of the taxes he examined. Their ratio of revenue to harm was low. His attitude towards the *customs duties* was unremittingly hostile. As the tables show, such taxes failed on almost all grounds. The only customs duties which found any favour with Norman were export duties. These could safely be levied within the limits of a country's competitive advantage.

He was slightly less hostile to *excise duties*, believing them to be more clearly confined to the purpose of raising revenue, rather than having purposes which he found less desirable, although in truth a number of them were actually sumptuary taxes, a purpose to which he had earlier objected. A further recommendation from Norman's point of view was that such taxes often fell on what he called a 'monopoly'. By this he meant that the good or service was supplied under conditions of less than perfect elasticity, so that there was, potentially at least, an intra-marginal surplus which could be abstracted without affecting price at the margin and thus, he believed, avoiding interference with the allocation of resources.

Customs and excise duties were, it was true, popular. This, despite his earlier requirement of popularity, did nothing to redeem them, in Norman's

---

[12]This section may have been inserted at Overstone's suggestion. It is not clear from his Ms comment on the *Essay* whether Overstone is making this as a fresh point, or merely commenting on an existing passage of the *Essay*.

eyes. Their popularity simply showed that taxpayers were mistaken. Welfare was, it emerges, not self perceived, in Norman's view. It was not, apparently, for taxpayers to evaluate their own loss of welfare from the tax system. Though Norman emphasised at a number of points in the *Essay* that individuals knew better than governments about the best allocation of resources, he was not prepared to accept that they knew best about their own welfare. In this he was true to the Utilitarian outlook.

He dismissed quickly *taxes on particular classes and persons*; these distorted the allocation of resources, and resulted in a welfare loss which he judged to be significantly greater than the gain to the revenue. He was less critical of the so-called 'Assessed Taxes', those on things like horses, windows, servants, and carriages. But such taxes were clumsy, and involved substantial collection and compliance costs. As the tables show, they thus failed under a number of Norman's headings.

In chapter 21 Norman argued that taxes on *travelling*, again despite their popularity, had nothing whatever to recommend them apart from simplicity and low compliance costs. They interfered with the functioning of the market, and fell on the more active and intelligent. In chapter 29 he considered turnpike and bridge tolls, and other duties of this kind. While he advanced no additional objections to these, it is noteworthy that he believed that charging travellers on the road was significantly superior to paying for roads out of general taxation – once government got its hands upon the revenue from roads, it would be spent on other things than travel. In the light of twentieth century British fiscal history, this was a prophetic statement indeed (Daunton, 2002, pp. 130-131).

Following Bentham (to whom he does not however refer), Norman was sharply critical of *law taxes*. Perhaps influenced, nonetheless, by the highly charged tone of Bentham's *A Protest Against Law Taxes*, Norman's criticisms are notably sharper than those he makes of other taxes.[13] They were, he

---

[13] Given the quotation from Norman's *Autobiography* at the head of this introduction to

argued, a premium on injustice, quite apart from a wide range of other drawbacks apparent in the tables above. Yet in one sense the discussion is puzzling. As Norman's contemporaries were well aware, it was the outrageous charges by lawyers, protected by the very structure of the legal system, as classically satirised by W.S. Gilbert and Charles Dickens, that provided the real premium on injustice and a barrier to the righting of wrongs. Adam Smith, in the previous century, had been well aware that court charges were only a small part of a legal bill (1776, Vol. II, pp. 239-242).

However some taxes on law took the form of *stamp duties*; and Norman devotes chapter 23 to such taxes. Taxes on the transfer of property were particularly cruel and oppressive – here he was at one with Smith, whom he quoted – while taxes on newspapers and other printed matter interfered with socially beneficial activities, as did taxes on insurance (an area in which Norman was for long, and profitably, engaged, as his *Autobiography* relates). In chapter 27 he objected particularly to the *legacy duty* and the *probate duty* as operated, because the landed interest had succeeded in securing exemption for real property. The scale as operated was also highly regressive. But he believed that if real property had been included, and there had been a proportional and not a regressive scale, the probate duty could have been made a good tax, and amalgamated with the legacy duty. The latter had however one anomaly which Norman defended. Higher rates of legacy duty were charged on distant relatives and those who were not relatives, when they received an inheritance. Norman asserts that such a distinction is in conformity with his Utilitarian scheme, but does not attempt to justify this assertion.

---

the *Essay*, it may seem odd that Norman does not refer to Bentham. However, Bentham was violently hostile to religious belief (Steintrager, 1977, pp. 16-17), while Norman, as his *Autobiography* relates, was deeply distressed by the scepticism of Voltaire and Comte. It may well be that Norman, for all his attachment to Utilitarianism, found Bentham himself an unattractive individual. He must indeed have been well aware how Bentham and, especially, James Mill, had turned his friend George Grote into a dogmatic atheist.

Chapters 24 and 25 are concerned with a range of taxes on *property*; taxes on rent, tithes, the British land tax, the poor rate, and the house and window taxes. For the most part, Norman approves of these – in the case of *tithes*, very much more than most of his contemporaries. He believed, in the standard Ricardian manner, the tax on rent to be one on an intra-marginal surplus, ignoring the manifold objections to this (O'Brien, 2004, p. 299). But he differed from Ricardo himself, who had objected to the tithe on the grounds that it was in proportion to the gross and not the net produce; for Norman argued that tithe actually fell on rent by restricting the margins of cultivation, through restricting the population, as a result of causing the price of food to be higher than it otherwise would be.[14]

He was however prepared to concede that collecting tithe in kind, as a proportion of output, was both expensive and 'vexatious', and he believed that it should be commuted, though he suggests a corn rent rather than a money payment, which is puzzling unless he believed that this would provide stability of tax yield.

The *land tax* Norman regarded as satisfactory – like Smith, he believed that the passing of time had rendered its faults insignificant. He approved in chapter 25 of the *poor rate* (for the relief of distress), though he believed that it should be imposed on the owner and not the occupier, and of the *house tax*. In chapter 28, returning to the matter of the house tax, he solved the problem of mansions, where the rent would hardly be a good tax base because of the difficulty of letting them, by suggesting taxing them instead on an imputed return to the market value of the building and its site. However he objected to the *window tax* which interfered with the enjoyment of light and was thus 'corruptive' in that it offered an inducement to brick up windows.

In chapter 26 Norman expressed some sympathy for the *poll tax*, despite its inequality and the expense of collection. Relying on the standard Ricar-

---

[14]The reasoning here depends heavily upon the Ricardian model, in which the size of the population determines the margin of cultivation; see O'Brien (2004, pp. 44-48).

dian argument that a *tax on wage earners* would be passed on, in the form of a compensating rise in wages and, correspondingly in the Ricardian model, a fall in the general rate of profit, he was also untroubled by the inequality of such a tax, at least in the long run. Again relying on the Ricardian model, he believed, however, that the rise in wages would alter the relative values of different commodities, which would affect the welfare of consumers according to their tastes.[15]

Although Norman was professedly liberal, and in some respects distinctly to the left of many of his contemporaries, his attitude towards what he called '*taxes on vice*' was distinctly censorious. The vices which he had in mind, or at least those to which he referred explicitly, were simply those on gambling. As the tables show, he found such taxes deeply unsatisfactory, even though he accepted that they were simple, popular, and caused little in the way of compliance costs.

The final three chapters of the *Essay*, 31-33, deal respectively with Norman's favourable view of the history of the *income tax* in England, his suggestions for an improved *property tax* – this is the nub of his plan for a single tax – and, failing the implementation of his plan, proposals for *reform* of the existing tax system.

In chapter 31 Norman, in contrast to many of his contemporaries (O'Brien, 1999, Vols IV, V, VI, VII), expressed enthusiasm for the income tax which he referred to as being 'in some respects the best source of revenue that the skill of our financiers has ever yet devised'. He was dismissive of objections to the 'inquisitorial' nature of the tax, unlike writers such as McCulloch, and despite the fact that this 'inquisitorial nature' was a key factor in the unpopularity of the tax, an unpopularity so marked that Parliament not only demanded that the government should honour its commitment to abolish the tax at the end of the Napoleonic wars but even that the income tax records should be

---

[15]For an account of the Ricardian mechanisms referred to in the text see O'Brien (2004, pp. 296-297, 98-103, 141-142).

destroyed. At one stage he approved capitalisation of non-permanent income to secure equality in conformity with his Utilitarian criterion, though he later changed his mind on this, as he recounts in his *Autobiography*.[16]

Norman attributed his change of mind to objections by Henry Warburton and others, and stated that he came to this conclusion after discussing the issue with his fellow Bank director J.G. Hubbard. On the face of it this is rather puzzling. Hubbard was an advocate of differentiation, that is of charging lower rates of tax on temporary incomes (profits and earnings) as against permanent incomes (deriving from property). This was essentially a rough and ready way of securing equality, without the apparatus of capitalisation which, as McCulloch pointed out, would involve enormous difficulties in practice (McCulloch, 1845, pp. 127-129), though there were other grounds for supporting differentiation (O'Brien, 2004, pp. 303-305). The issue of differentiation was one hotly disputed by Norman's contemporaries (O'Brien, 1999, Vols IV, V, VI, VII) on a variety of grounds of varying degrees of subtlety. Warburton's argument however was a very simple one; under-declaration of temporary income ensured that it was taxed, as a whole, at a lower rate.

In chapter 32 we come to the core of Norman's programme – his ideal. He believed that the ideal tax system would involve a *single tax on property*. This would replace *all* other taxes. Such a tax would be levied in proportion to the value of property, in conformity with Norman's decision noted earlier to oppose progression. However it would, in the conventional Classical manner, be subject to a tax free 'subsistence minimum'. There would be general property registration to make levying of such a tax possible in practice, and the results would be made public. Norman believed that such a tax would have all the qualities to be desired in the best possible tax system. Difficulties, such as the fact that commercial capital had no value

---

[16]Such a scheme involved imputing an income to the capitalised value of the income stream, at an assumed rate of interest; see O'Brien (2004, pp. 320-322).

independent of the prospective income stream, were side-stepped. And an argument employed by Ricardo in support of a capital levy which exempted the professional classes was employed to suggest that there would be no harm if the professional classes were exempted from the proposed property tax. Ricardo argued that professional earnings would adjust downward so as to eliminate the tax advantage (see Ricardo, 1820; in O'Brien, 1999, Vol. III, p. 331). Such a tax would, in Norman's view be 'computable', 'economical', 'constant', 'divisible', 'non-interferent', and less 'corruptive' than the existing tax system.

In adopting this position, Norman exhibited the extraordinary confidence of the Benthamites (and indeed of liberal classes of all generations), that only prejudice and ignorance (and democracy) stood in the way of the implementation of their panaceas. None the less, he accepted that, because such unfortunate attitudes existed, it was necessary to put forward in chapter 33 a programme of tax reform which stopped short of the single tax solution.

He argued that government should reform the existing tax system by minimising public expenditure; by increasing what he judged to be the least harmful of the existing taxes; by introducing some new sources of revenue; and by using the scope which this provided to remove the taxes which he judged to be the most harmful.

The possibility of expenditure reductions assumed in chapter 33 provided room for manoeuvre. Without particularisation, Norman plucked from the air a figure of £2 million as the maximum safe reduction. On the revenue side he suggested extending and reforming the duties on inheritance, on the lines set out in chapter 27. Here, as earlier, he defends discrimination against more distant relatives in the levying of such a duty, and claims, without any attempt to substantiate the claim, that such discrimination is in accordance with his Utilitarian principles.

The window tax should be abolished, but the house tax should be reformed by removing the large number of exceptions which had grown up.

Discrimination against Baltic timber in the levying of timber duties (a personal grievance) should be abolished and 'a very light property tax', only levied on real property and financial securities, should be introduced. Traders and professional men would pay a fixed sum per annum instead of the tax.

Norman calculated that all these measures would produce a surplus of £9.5 million. With this in hand the stamp duties on insurance, deeds, law proceedings, bills of exchange, and newspapers could be abolished together with a wide range of duties on things like stage coaches, paper, and advertisements. In addition the duty on tea and sugar could be reduced, the duties on malt and glass reformed, and customs and excise lowered to the point where smuggling was not worthwhile.

Once the thin end of the wedge of a 'very light' property tax had been introduced, Norman believed that it should be increased 'as fast as circumstances might allow'.

Conclusion

It would be foolish to claim that Norman's *Essay* is a finished product, without inconsistencies and misconceptions. But as a piece of applied Benthamism it is of considerable interest. It is much to be regretted that Norman's diffidence did not allow him to publish it, because consequent criticism might have allowed him to combine a welfare analysis with an approach which laid more stress on economic growth as an objective. This could have been very fruitful.

It is clear, however that, in his *Essay*, Norman placed far too much faith in the willingness of governments to control expenditure rigorously, and he clung tenaciously to the idea that his proposed single tax would be adequate to meet all the revenue needs of government. For tax reform did not move British public finances towards a single tax, but towards greater government expenditure. Peel, though despised by Norman, as his *Autobiography* shows, introduced in 1842 a programme of tax reform which had much in common with Norman's own prescriptions.[17]

This included the re-introduction of the income tax, so favoured by Norman. Successive Chancellors of the Exchequer then strove to abolish this tax which had been re-introduced by Peel as an avowedly temporary measure in the face of an anticipated short-fall of revenue, following the removal of many duties. In this, in the face of civil service resistance, they failed. But, instead of the income tax being a sole tax, and supplying all the government's revenue needs, with expenditure rigorously controlled, as Norman envisaged, it became the fulcrum of a large and steady increase in the range of government activities, an increase so large that the income tax had to be supplemented by a wide range of other duties. Indeed one of Norman's contemporaries, Sir Samuel Morton Peto, pointed out that the income tax had become an engine of increasing government expenditure (Peto, 1863; in O'Brien, 1999, Vol. VII, p. 90).

It is instructive to see that this is exactly how Overstone, Norman's close intellectual ally, was later to view a desirable tax system, in a memorandum prepared in 1860. He believed that no single tax could produce equality – which, like Norman, he interpreted as 'leaving the different classes of the community in the same condition relatively to each other in which they would be were there no Taxation'.[18]

No single tax could achieve this. A whole range of taxes had to be employed in order to achieve justice. An income tax (and note that this is Overstone's preference, rather than a property tax as favoured by Norman) should form a part of a general system of taxation. A permanent income tax, as part of a general system of taxation, so that different classes were taxed in different ways, was an entirely valid revenue tool in Overstone's view. Once it

---

[17]For details both of the budget of 1842 and of the financial situation facing Peel, see Stafford Northcote (1862, pp. 1-48).

[18]Overstone's document is reproduced in O'Brien (1971, Vol. III, pp. 1470-1474). The original is in the Overstone papers.

was made permanent (and he believed this to have been Peel's real intention when introducing a 'temporary' income tax in 1842) most of the arguments relating to such a tax would cease to be of importance. This was especially true of those relating to the taxation of temporary and permanent incomes, which would under such circumstances be taxed permanently or temporarily, and thus the question of differentiation would not arise.

Yet Norman, who lived to see the development of such a system may, despite the arguments in the *Essay*, have been not entirely unhappy about the development. Not only does the *Essay* begin with tributes to taxation and government as marks of civilisation, but in his 1850 work on taxation he had so far moved from his calls for economy that he favoured increased government expenditure.

In the 1850 publication, which Norman revised in successive editions (the fourth edition appeared in 1864), he managed to deal with a wide range of issues, in an impressive and assured manner. In this, in contrast to his advocacy of expenditure reductions in the *Essay*, Norman argued that there was plenty of scope for increasing public expenditure. He believed British public expenditure to be modest in comparison with that of other countries. Indeed he set out to counter three beliefs which Norman believed to be widespread. Firstly that public expenditure hindered economic growth; secondly that British public expenditure was high in relation to national income; and, thirdly, that successive British governments were characterised by financial extravagance. He used population data, provided by the successive censuses, as a proxy measure of national income, then argued that national income per head had increased significantly since 1815. Norman was thus able to argue that Britain had enjoyed economic growth. Relating his estimate of national income to figures of government expenditure, he was satisfied that the ratio of public expenditure to national income had fallen since 1815. He compared tax burdens in Britain and France, and concluded that the French taxpayer was much more heavily taxed than the British one. Finally he argued that, allowing for the fact that Britain had very large defence commitments but did not, unlike other countries, use conscription, the level of public expenditure was actually low. This gave him the opportunity to argue for greater government expenditure, notably on education.

However it is the *Essay*, Norman's personal fusion of Utilitarianism and Classical economics, with which we are concerned here. As a product of its time and the intellectual environment, it provides some insight into the concerns of the liberal and indeed of the radical classes on the pressing issues of raising a sufficient tax revenue in the years after 1815, and it is worth studying.

D.P. O'Brien

Bibliography

[1] Bentham, J. (1843) *Works* (Ed. by J. Bowring). Edinburgh: Tait; London: Simkin and Marshall.

[2] Cohen-Stuart, A.J. (1958) On Progressive Taxation. Trans. by J.C. Te Velde. In *Classics in the Theory of Public Finance* (Ed. by R.A. Musgrave and A.T. Peacock). London: Macmillan.

[3] Daunton, M. (2002) *Just Taxes: The Politics of Taxation in Britain, 1914-1979*. Cambridge: Cambridge University Press.

[4] McCulloch, J.R. (1845) *A Treatise on the Principles and Practical Influence of Taxation and the Funding System*. 3rd edition 1863. (Ed. by D.P. O'Brien). Edinburgh: Scottish Academic Press for the Scottish Economic Society.

[5] Mill, J.S. (1848) *Principles of Political Economy with Some of their Applications to Social Philosophy*. 7th edition, 1871. (Ed. by W.J. Ashley). London: Longmans (1923).

[6] Norman, G.W. (1850) *An Examination of Some Prevailing Opinions, as to the Pressure of Taxation in This, and Other Countries*. 4th edition. London: T.&W. Boone (1864).

[7] Northcote, H.S. (1862) *Twenty Years of Financial Policy*. London: Saunders, Otley.

[8] O'Brien, D.P. (1970) *J.R. McCulloch. A Study in Classical Economics.* Reprinted London: Routledge (2003).

[9] O'Brien, D.P. (ed.) (1971) *The Correspondence of Lord Overstone.* 3 vols. Cambridge: Cambridge University Press.

[10] O'Brien, D.P. (ed.) (1999) *The History of Taxation.* 8 vols. London: Pickering and Chatto.

[11] O'Brien, D.P. (2004) *The Classical Economists Revisited.* Princeton: Princeton University Press.

[12] Ricardo, D. (1821) *On the Principles of Political Economy and Taxation.* 3rd edition. Vol. I. of *The Works and Correspondence of David Ricardo* (Ed. by P. Sraffa). Cambridge: Cambridge University Press (1951).

[13] Smith, A. (1776) *An Inquiry into the Nature and Causes of the Wealth of Nations.* (Ed. by E. Cannan, 1904). reprinted London: Methuen (1961).

[14] Stark, W. (ed.) (1952) *Jeremy Bentham's Economic Writings.* London: Allen and Unwin for the Royal Economic Society.

[15] Steintrager, J. (1977) *Bentham.* London: Allen and Unwin.

Essay on Taxation

Part I

Introduction

Chapter 1

Political Economy and Taxation

Among the several branches of science connected with the political and social relations of man there are few more interesting than that which explains the true principles of taxation, and scarcely any more generally neglected. Its importance requires no laboured proof, for the universal testimony of Nations points out taxation as one of the causes, which affect most materially the public happiness. Its evils are complained of in the pages of the annalist of every age and country, and the murmurs of the People shew that in this instance History tells the truth. Yet, notwithstanding this general agreement, few attempts have been made to subject this department of Science, which were it allowable to coin a new word, might be denominated 'Fiscality' to a rigorous and searching analysis, which should place its principles on a firm basis, and explain their practical application.

The connexion between Political Economy, and a correct theory of taxation is so intimate, that it was manifestly impossible to make any progress in the latter while the former was unknown or in its infancy; and it was not therefore to be expected that any writers anterior to A. Smith, even had they felt the importance of the Subject, and turned their attention to it, could have laid down a set of principles, calculated to guide the Legislator, in the construction of a financial system. Had the attempt indeed been made, it would infallibly have failed. A. Smith when he erected Political Economy

into a Science, founded not on arbitrary assumptions, but on a legitimate
induction from facts, was naturally led to cast a glance on the effects of taxation; he could hardly do more in consequence of the wide and general scope
of his work – and the result of his reasoning on the subject, is given in the
four rules which he lays down at the commencement of the second part – lst
Chapter Book 5 and subsequently explains. His maxims are for the most part
correct, but imperfectly arranged, and far less extensive than the subject to
which they apply.[1]

The followers of A. Smith, so far as taxation is concerned, have added but
little to his discoveries. Their object has generally been to treat exclusively
of the production, distribution, and consumption of wealth, and this did not
allow them to examine thoroughly, and in all its details, a matter which
in one direction formed only a small part of their subject, and in another
extended far beyond its limits.

Their plan thus obliged them to take a one-sided and imperfect view of
taxation. They regarded it almost exclusively, as affecting the riches of the
State or of individuals, they discussed it economically either passing over
altogether its moral effects, or only casting on them a hasty and superficial
glance. Those who will examine the works of Ricardo, of McCulloch, Say,
Storch &c. will be convinced how much these eminent writers have left
undone, and even unattempted in this branch of human knowledge.[2]

---

[1] [Adam Smith *An Inquiry into the Nature and Causes of the Wealth of Nations* (1776)
ed. E. Cannan (1904), reprinted London: Methuen, 1961. Book V, 'Of the Revenue of the
Sovereign or Commonwealth', pp. 213-486, Chapter 2, Part II, 'Of Taxes', pp. 349-352.
Smith's four maxims were Equality, Certainty, Convenience of Payment, and Economy in
Collection. As pointed out in the Introduction, these maxims proved central to Norman's
own understanding of tax principles.]

[2] [Although Norman started this *Essay*, according to his own account, late in 1821, and
although he was leading discussions of its central question at the Political Economy Club
in early 1822 (see note 3, p. 184), it is very clear that he returned to the *Essay* many times
in subsequent years, revising it. The date of this comment is thus uncertain. The first
edition of McCulloch's *The Principles of Political Economy with a Sketch of the Rise and
Progress of the Science* (Edinburgh and London: Tait) did not appear until 1825, though
he had been writing on economics since 1816 (D.P. O'Brien *J.R. McCulloch: A Study
in Classical Economics*. London: Allen and Unwin, 1970, reprinted London: Routledge,

The work of Sir H. Parnell on financial reform points more directly than theirs to the same object as the author's, and has been of essential service, by popularizing correct opinions on several important matters. The chief fault consists in a neglect of the moral effects of taxation.[3]

The object of the present work is to supply, in some degree, the deficiencies of the above distinguished writers, to do that which they would have done much better had they aimed at doing it.

In the following Treatise it is intended to reject everything extraneous, to the simple object of showing how a given sum may be levied on a Nation, with the least sacrifice on the part of the tax-payers.

The mode adopted for carrying this plan into effect, is in the first place to describe those qualities which it is desirable, that any single impost, or a whole system of imposts should possess. Secondly – To examine various existing or supposeable taxes, with a view to discover, whether they possess

2003, p. 70). It is the *Principles* which Norman is most likely to have in mind, given that he is referring to systematic treatises but, prior to the appearance of that book, the bulk of McCulloch's output had either been anonymous (as was the case with his Edinburgh Review articles) and/or of limited circulation (as in the case of the Scotsman). The first edition of McCulloch's *Treatise on Taxation* did not appear until 1845, though it incorporated a good deal of material dating from his earlier writings, some of it (as in the case of material from the Scotsman) from very much earlier. See J.R. McCulloch *A Treatise on the Principles and Practical Influence of Taxation and the Funding System* (1845) ed. D.P.O'Brien, Edinburgh: Scottish Academic Press, 1975 . H.F. v. Storch (1766-1835) was a little known figure even at that date, though the erudite McCulloch knew of him, who had produced historical and statistical work on Russia. However he was the author of a general work on economics , The *Cours d'Economie Politique* (St Petersburg: A. Pluchart, 1815), and of a work on public finance *Considérations sur la Nature du Revenu Natural* (Paris: Bossange, 1824). Judging from his comment, Norman may not have known of this work. The edition of the *Cours* which he knew may well have been the one published by Ailland in Paris in 1823, with notes by J.B. Say, rather than the St Petersburg edition. The work by Say himself which Norman would have had in mind was the *Traité d'Economie Politique*, which first appeared in 1803. However, a subsequent reference suggests that the edition used by Norman was the fifth edition in three volumes published by Rapilly in Paris in 1826. The straightforward case is Ricardo. The first edition of his *Principles* appeared in 1817, the third in 1821, and he was known to, and appreciated by, Norman. See D. Ricardo *On the Principles of Political Economy and Taxation* ed. P. Sraffa, Cambridge: Cambridge University Press, 1951.]

[3] [Sir Henry Parnell *On Financial Reform*, London: J. Murray, 1830, third edition 1831. Norman refers to this work at several points in his *Essay*.]

at all, or to what extent the several desirable qualities. Thirdly – To explain what seems to be the least objectionable mode of supplying the pecuniary wants of the Government, in accordance with the principles previously laid down.

Taxation may be levied on persons, property, talents, knowledge &c, and property may be abstracted either in kind or in money. In order thoroughly to exhaust the subject, it would be necessary to discuss separately each of these modes of taking from individuals a portion of what belongs to them for State purposes, but even an attempt to do so, would extend this work to an inconvenient bulk, and it has therefore been determined to consider all taxes as paid in money, unless where some other mode of payment is specified. This will simplify the subject, and reduce it to manageable dimensions, while the conclusions arrived at, may easily be transferred by the reader, mutatis mutandis, to any other mode of payment.

Nobody can be more thoroughly aware than the author, that his task has been imperfectly performed. It was begun and great progress was made in it many years ago since which time discoveries in science have completely changed, or at least modified conclusions previously arrived at; hence has followed the necessity of numerous alterations and additions; which have affected the unity and completeness of the whole, and rendered it a piece of patchwork of which the several parts may in some instances exhibit incongruity instead of harmony. It can hardly be expected to become popular, because it appeals not to the passions or prejudices, not to the idols which lead men astray, but to their reason, and aims at producing conviction, not amusement. In this respect it might perhaps have been improved, by a more frequent use of examples and illustrations, but these would have swelled to a great bulk, and it seemed desirable to make a sacrifice for the sake of brevity. If however, as the author firmly believes, his principles are for the most part true in themselves, and correctly applied, he cannot but entertain a hope, that they will make their way in spite of the garb they wear, among a few enquiring minds: and that persons will be found better skilled in the difficult art of book-making than himself, to bring them forward in a more attractive dress, and thus obtain the public attention for a most important branch of human knowledge, which appears at present little else than a Terra incognita; of which even to the learned, only the coasts and a few elevated points are known. Even should his principles and their application be deemed altogether erroneous, he may still have the satisfaction of awakening the attention, and directing the researches of more powerful minds to a subject equally interesting to the Philosopher and the man of the world, to the Statesman who wields the destinies of Nations, and the people who submit to his guidance.

Chapter 2

Advantages of Taxation

Before we proceed to what constitutes the real object of this Essay, an investigation of the qualities which ought to belong to a tax, and an analysis of various imposts with a view of pointing out in what degree, if at all, they possess these qualities, it will be desirable to say a few words upon the nature and effects of taxation in general. Taxation is a word to which unfavourable associations are attached; in many parts and ages of the world, it has been almost synonymous with robbery and plunder, and at best it betokens a sacrifice on the part of him, who is called upon to pay it, of a portion of those means of enjoyment which fortune or his own industry have procured for him. Still even in its rudest shape, it implies an advance into the domain of civilization, a state elevated above absolute barbarism, for without it, there can be no approach to a regular government, nothing in the shape of an union where persons and property are even imperfectly protected from internal and external foes. A few scattered families or even tribes of savages may exist without any thing like public contributions, but these must have been almost co-existent with the foundation of all political Societies.

Taxation is a necessary consequence of a combination and division of labor as applied to Governments. Instead of each person performing every service for himself, it is found more advantageous, that a small number of individuals should be employed to perform certain services for the whole community.

These persons sooner or later must be remunerated by the State.

A. Smith first pointed out the influence of the division of labour on the productive powers of industry, but its effects are no less important and beneficial in the business of the State than in that of the factory.

It is plain that the very notion of Government implies the existence of a set of persons employed in the discharge of duties necessary or beneficial to the public at large. Now these in order to exist must be nominated in general only for a short period, so as to leave them sufficient time for the management of their own affairs, and be succeeded by others, to be subsequently replaced; or they must be paid for their services. The result in the first case is partial Taxation applied to the time and talents of individuals, in the second case, where the principle of a division of labour is more perfectly developed, it is a general contribution either of money or money's worth, employed in the payment of salaries. In all countries, elevated above absolute barbarism, taxation exists in both shapes, but the first becomes less and less generally applicable, as the size of political unions increases, as mankind becomes numerous and rich, and their relations augment in number and importance until at length, except in the shape of a military conscription, it chiefly appears in the discharge of certain municipal offices, of trifling labour and importance, the duties of which, after all, might usually be better performed by salaried functionaries, devoting their whole time to public business.

The Artisan who in a rude state of society joins together many trades, will probably excel in none, he will produce but little, and that little will be of bad quality. The same consequence will be found to result from filling the offices of Government with men, not trained to them by education and habit, but summoned for a time from their usual avocations upon which their thoughts are fixed, and to which they are eager to return. It cannot be denied, but that the Judge, the Soldier, the Minister, or the Legislator who receives from the State a sum sufficient for his maintenance, who has undergone a regular course of instruction, and who devotes his whole time and energies, to the discharge of his official duties, must perform them, in nine cases out of ten, much better than the person who is casually chosen to supply his place.

By the second plan, that of paying salaries in exact analogy with the economic effects produced by the division of labour on the production of commodities, not only is the business of the State better, but it is also more cheaply done; the sacrifices imposed by the taxes required to pay appropriate salaries are much less than would be required according to the first plan, whereby individuals would be called upon to contribute in person instead of in purse. The Farmer would be summoned from his plough, the Merchant from his counting house to fight the enemy, or to decide causes. Certain Public Offices would demand from those who filled them a long absence from their usual residences. If the selection to these were made by lot, it might be said that no injustice was committed, but the necessary effect might be, the very extremity of distress to whole families, while the uncertainty as to the individuals upon whom the burdens might fall, would fill every breast with anxiety and consternation. Should the offices in question be filled by election, an intolerable grievance would be imposed on talents, knowledge, and virtue, and every body would avoid the acquisition of such dangerous and costly possessions. A general impost employed in the purchase of the required services must occasion a much less sacrifice than this arbitrary system.

In some instances it will be found that the gratification of ambition or vanity, or of a more laudable zeal for the common good, may afford a sufficient stimulus to the acceptance of public office, and an adequate discharge of their duties. In such cases, a wise Government would not assign them salaries, taking care however, that the duties in question were really well performed, which practically speaking they rarely are under the circumstances supposed. We often see important services altogether neglected, or imperfectly discharged, by a functionary who perhaps from a feeling of parsimony is unpaid, when the loss arising from his misconduct, occasions a sacrifice infinitely greater than the amount of any salary that would be required, to secure the exertions of a person, properly qualified.

More arguments might be adduced upon this important subject but enough it may be hoped has been said to prove, that so far from being an evil, taxation confined within due bounds, discreetly levied, and well applied, is one of the most useful institutions that the wit of man, has ever yet devised, when considered merely with a view to the payment of those employed in the simple and necessary duties of Government. Setting aside its other good effects, it even thus far adds greatly to the National Wealth, instead of diminishing it.

But the payment of salaries to those who make laws, who decide disputes, or punish offenders, or who expose their lives in contending against foreign enemies, or in suppressing internal tumult is not the only useful purpose to which a public revenue may be applied. The facilitating communications will require the establishment of roads, canals, harbours &c. &c. and in a new country, especially where capitals are small, the risk of such undertakings is great, and the profit distant, it may be proper that the Government itself should construct them, taking due care to leave them to individuals, whenever it may be practicable so to do. Forts, prisons &c &c will also be required and all these objects of expenditure, under a proper system of management, will add to, instead of diminishing the National wealth. An attempt will be made hereafter to shew that the conveyance of letters is likewise a public service, which ought to be, or at least might advantageously be defrayed by a general tax.

Another object, which in most, if not all countries, requires to be assisted from the financial resources of the State, is education. Ignorance produces the greater portion of all the misery that exists upon earth. Its removal or diminution essentially interests the wellbeing of the whole community; in some instances the poor have not the pecuniary means of securing the blessings of knowledge to their children, in others schools are wanting altogether, or if in existence their quality is so bad, as to render them little better than useless.

It need hardly be mentioned that the maintenance of churches and ministers, and religious instruction in general may require succours from the State, when without such support the public wants in this respect would be imperfectly supplied.

The last object, which need be mentioned, as authorizing under certain circumstances disbursements from the public revenues, is relief to indigence. This may be afforded either in the shape of hospitals, of occasional gifts to lessen the pressure of any accidental calamity &c &c. or as the English poor rates which it seems clear might be so managed as to relieve more misery than they create.

From all that has been said it will appear incontestably that taxation is the unavoidable accompaniment of an organised Government, that the idea of the one, is as it were involved in that of the other, & that the amount of the latter, when confined within due bounds, is the necessary price we pay for the advantages resulting from the former. It should be the endeavour of a wise legislature, to reduce this price to a minimum by:

1. Maintaining no larger a number of public servants than are absolutely necessary;

2. Never giving higher salaries, than may be sufficient to secure the services of functionaries adequately qualified;

3. Employing the incentive of honor as a reward, whenever it can be usefully substituted for that of gain;

4. Levying the sum, which after the application of the above rules, may still be required for the use of the State in such a way as may occasion the smallest possible diminution of the general happiness.

The three first of these maxims will be only occasionally alluded to in the following essay. A searching explanation of the last, forms its peculiar object, and the result will be to show the possibility of curing, under that head alone, a large proportion of the evils that ordinarily flow from fiscal exactions.

It would form a very interesting disquisition to give a sort of hypothetical history of taxation; to trace its progress from the rude levies of fish or game, differing little from mere robbery, made upon his followers by the chief of some petty-tribe, through the ill-contrived exactions of the Satrap, the Pasha, and the Feudal Baron whose emoluments are mixed up with the tribute of money or military service yielded to the sovereign, to the complicated and artificial systems of finance adapted by polished Nations. To observe how in many countries the revenue of the Chief of the State as a great proprietor, blends into those which he exacts from his subjects for purposes of Government, and finally to illustrate the discussion by a reference to the practice of mankind, as evinces in the descriptions of historians and travellers of all ages and countries. But such a disquisition however interesting would form an excrescence to the present work, with which it has no necessary connexion and would swell it beyond all reasonable bounds, thus adding to a fault, which will perhaps be justly reproached to it even in its present state.

Part II

Qualities of Taxation

Chapter 3

Taxes and Other Sources of Revenue

In the introduction an attempt was made to prove that taxation is a necessary concomitant of Government, but that, as under the most favourable circumstances it always involves a diminution of the means of procuring happiness in those who pay it, every wise & honest legislature is bound to lessen as far as possible the sacrifices thus occasioned.

The effects of taxation may be considered under several points of view:

1. As to its amount whether too large or too small or just sufficient for the purposes of good government;

2. As to the mode of its application;

3. As to the manner in which it is levied.

The present enquiry will be confined to the last head. The others would belong more properly to a general disquisition on government.

It has been often asserted, that, the best plan of finance is that which requires the least revenue, and the best tax that, which raises the smallest sum from the people.[1] If this be considered as a mere general recommendation of

---

[1]'Le meilleur de tous les plans de finance est de depénser peu, et le meilleur de tous les impôts est le plus petit' – Say Traité d'Economie Politique Vol. 3, p. 153. ['The best

economy it may be pardoned, but if it be meant to direct the operations of the Statesman, its incorrectness is palpable, for of two taxes which diminish in an exactly equal degree the enjoyments of a Nation, which oppose the same obstacles to production and accumulation one may bring £1,000,000 into the exchequer, and another only half the sum, one may afford only a slight stimulus to crime, another may demoralize a Province. This being indubitably the case, as will appear when we examine the various modes of taxation now in use, it becomes necessary in order to frame such a fiscal system as may yield the sum required for the public service, with the least loss of public happiness, to enumerate and define those qualities which it is so desirable a tax should possess. Thus we shall require an act of general principles, and if the reasons on which they are founded, be clear and conclusive, we shall be able to apply them with confidence to every particular case. We shall possess as it were, a set of scales in which the comparative excellence of any given tax may be easily weighed.

It is almost unnecessary to observe that what is said of one tax in particular may be extended to all, to each component of the heterogeneous mass of contributions which fills the exchequer of most civilized countries. The effects produced by the levying a tax upon the well being of the community may be considered under two comprehensive points of view:

1. As it diminishes the means of enjoyment, previously possessed by calling on each individual or the community at large, to resign a portion of his wealth;

2. As it affords an incentive to crime, falls unequally upon particular

---

of all plans of finance is to spend little, and the best of all taxes is the smallest.' See J.B. Say *Traité d'Economie Politique, ou Simple Exposition de la Manière dont se Forment, se Distribuent, et se Consomment les Richesses.* 3 Vols, Paris: Rapilly, 1826, Vol. III, p. 153. See also J.B. Say *A Treatise on Political Economy* trans. C.R. Prinsep, reprinted New York: A.M. Kelley, 1971 p. 449.]

classes or particular persons or excites terror or anxiety, dispropor-
tioned to its amount.

In the first case a diminution of public happiness is occasioned indirectly through the medium of wealth, which is one of the most efficient means of procuring it. In the second the happiness of the community is directly affected. The first class may be called the economical, the second the moral effects of taxation.

The evils which any given tax may inflict on the individuals who pay it, or the community at large, may extend to almost every source of human happiness; it may affect the persons of men, their reputation, their fortune, their condition, their social affections, their moral qualities &c &c, and that with an almost endless difference in intensity, and its consequences may be still further diversified by the peculiar circumstances which belong to each separate person. Considerable difficulties therefore present themselves in an attempt to classify these various phenomena.

In the present section the principal evils which can afflict mankind taking taxation for their source, will be thrown into classes with a constant view to completeness, precision and brevity. In this task however after all his exertion the author has failed to satisfy even himself, still less can he hope to satisfy his readers.

By some the qualities, that is to say the classes of human evils, which have been selected, will be considered too numerous, by others they will be thought too few, by a third party the points of resemblance which connect the particulars contained in each class will be blamed as badly selected & the distribution will be called faulty. Differences of opinion on this part of a very difficult and complicated subject can hardly fail to arise; at any rate a new & important path, hitherto almost untrod, will be opened to the investigations of intelligent men.

It must not indeed be supposed, that a thoroughly distinct line can in all cases be drawn between the different characteristic qualities. In many instances the possession of one, so necessarily supposes that of another, that it is difficult to consider them separately, in others they follow and blend into each other, by such insensible gradations, that it is almost impossible to say where one ends and the other begins. In the moral as in the physical world, nature refuses to lend herself to our artificial distinctions, and bursts through her fetters however skilfully they may be fabricated.

It will be assumed throughout the following section that the minimum of evil which a tax can inflict, unless in one or two cases which will be specified, is the loss of the happiness which might be purchased by its amount plus the smallest cost of collection. This follows from the definition of a tax, a contribution either in commodities, or services, corporeal, or mental, levied on its subject by the sovereign or the governing body. For the sake of distinctness and because the fact generally is so, it is here usually regarded as being paid in money which may afterwards be exchanged for the commodities or services of which the Government may stand in need.

In some countries as in China, a very large part of the whole revenues, and in all some part, either general or local is paid in kind. The proportion so paid will usually vary inversely with the increase of civilization. It appears unnecessary to examine particularly the effects produced by the payment of taxes in kind, because an attentive consideration of the desirable qualities will enable the reader to perceive in what cases and to what extent such a practice should be allowed to exist; and it will suffice at present to remark that, speaking generally, levies in money possess all the advantages over those in kind, both for the people and the Government, which are exhibited in the state of commerce as carried on in a civilized country over the barter which supplies its place among a tribe of savages.

There are some sources of revenue not falling under the above definition of a tax, though called in popular language by the same name, which deserve attention. Their striking peculiarity is that they are in one instance paid by nobody, in others not by the subjects of the legislature imposing them.[2] It is obvious therefore that they should be resorted to, exclusively, whenever the amount they are capable of yielding suffices for the general purposes of the State, and as far as they will go, when a larger amount is required. They are as follows:

1. A monopoly of some particular article of produce received from property belonging, to the State. Such would have been a portion of gold or silver retained from the Mexican mines, supposing that they had belonged to the King of Spain, and that the precious metals had been found no where else. This is a case which may be imagined, but can hardly exist to a sufficient extent to be of much practical importance.

2. Rent – when originally appropriated by the Sovereign, as in India and other Eastern Countries an impost on rent in Europe where the Land has become the property of private persons, falls within our definition.

3. Duties on commodities exported – these in all cases fall on the foreigner who consumes the taxed commodity except when the produce of a monopoly. They may indeed be carried so high as to render the article exported dearer than some home commodity, or than the produce of a third country calculated to supply its place, in which case the exportation must cease. The skill of the legislator must therefore confine the duty within proper bounds.

4. Tribute from foreign States. Some of these several sources of revenue will be frequently alluded to in the following pages.

The above introductory remarks will clear the way for a separate description of each of those qualities, which are calculated to reduce to a minimum

---

[2]Ricardo Pol Econ [The reference is to David Ricardo *Principles of Political Economy and Taxation* Vol. I in *The Works and Correspondence of David Ricardo* ed. P. Sraffa, Cambridge: Cambridge University Press, 1951, pp. 173, 181, 194-200, 240.]

the evils resulting from any given tax. In executing this task, from the novelty of the subject, it will be necessary to make use of certain terms in a restricted sense, or with a meaning affixed to them somewhat different from that in which they are usually employed. This is our evil certainly, but an evil which, under the circumstances of the case, is unavoidable. An evil equally unavoidable, and for which an apology once for all is now made, will appear in the occasional repetition of some fact or argument. The origin of this apparent fault lies chiefly in three sources:

1. The similarity in some respects of things, which differ under other points of view;

2. The necessity of citing and referring to particular instances, in the establishment and elucidation of general principles; which particular instances, or others analogous to them, must be subsequently examined when the general principles are applied;

3. A wish to diminish, as much as possible, the number of references.

Chapter 4

Computability

A tax is called computable when the sum it will produce, and all its other effects can be exactly predicted beforehand. The perfection of computability would take place, supposing that every man's income and property were accurately known, and a tax imposed of a given proportion, which the collector should call to receive on a certain day previously announced. The whole amount of privation imposed could then be expressed in numerical figures. It is obviously impossible to form a perfect opinion of the effects of any measure upon public happiness, unless we are acquainted with all the nice ramifications of consequences, both direct and indirect, which it is calculated to produce; in proportion to the exactitude of our previous knowledge as to these effects, will be our power of forming a measure suitable to the object in view. Perfect computability is practicably unattainable, an approximation to it is all that can be realized. In order to be able to pronounce that a tax is computable, the following questions must be answered satisfactorily.

1. Can the amount it will yield, the time of receipt and the expense of collection be exactly foreseen?

2. Can the legislature predict upon whom it will fall and in what proportion?

3. Can it produce any other contingent effects, direct, or indirect, than

those intended, and what are they?

It must always be kept in view, that a tax should be computable not merely as respects the Government but also as respects the payers.

Unless a tax possess the quality in question we are obviously unable to know, in what degree the other desirable qualities belong to it, for these qualities are merely names given to the modes in which it affects public happiness. In order that a tax should be computable, it is necessary that the lawgiver should have accurate information as to the number, situation and fortune of the persons who are to pay it, supposing it to be levied in proportion to wealth, or as to the numerical amount or value, or both, of the objects exposed to it, supposing it to fall on commodities or actions. Now the population of a country may be readily ascertained with accuracy. The general wealth of individuals is open, though less easily to observation and valuation, especially that which consists in fixed property; but the amount of commodities which are frequently produced and consumed, or of actions performed, viewed either separately or in mass, is perpetually changing; they are liable to vary from an infinite variety of causes, and all imposts upon them must be therefore deficient in the quality of computability. Who can foresee how many barrels of beer, or how many quarters of malt will be produced in Great Britain during the ensuing year, or how many pounds of tea, or Cwt. of sugar will be imported or who will consume these several articles. Even could this be ascertained, exactly only half the work would be done, for it would still be necessary to know how each consumer might be affected, by the rise of price, in the objects he desired to purchase. The tax would be computable with respect to the Government but not with respect to the payers.

Experience shews that an increase in the rate of duty, is rarely if ever followed by an equal proportionate increase in the revenue received, and often by an absolute diminution. Thus then, even in a financial point of view, such increased taxes in the instances referred to, have been wholly sufficient, the exchequer would probably have been richer had they never existed, but unfortunately, as we shall subsequently find, the privation of enjoyment which the money paid in a tax might have procured is only one, and frequently the least of the evils it occasions. It may sometimes diminish the revenue, and yet inflict an enormous sacrifice on the community.[1]

If it be granted, that, as the amount of the greater number of commodities is perpetually varying, they can never form the subject of a really computable tax. Though in this respect some may afford superior advantages to others, it remains to be seen whether property or income do not more nearly approximate to perfection in this respect, such property or income being valued and registered previously to the imposition of the tax. This operation would be highly desirable for other reasons besides its subserviency to the establishment of a good plan of finance; through its means almost all disputes as to the title to property would be wholly avoided; a source of enormous roguery, expense and litigation would be abolished, and a ready solution would be obtained of some of the most difficult problems in political science, which are now rendered doubtful from the want of data, necessary for their elucidation.

The remainder of the chapter will be chiefly devoted to the discussion of this important point, and the result will be to shew, that the obstacles to a registration have been greatly exaggerated, and that it would be very possible to establish a system sufficiently exact for all practical purposes. All property is either fixed or circulating; in the first class are included, land, houses the national debt, and every thing else which from its nature cannot be removed, or escape observation; the distribution of all wealth of this kind may of course

[1] For instances see Sir H. Parnell Finl. Refm, p.37 et seq. [The reference is to Sir Henry Parnell *On Financial Reform*, London: J. Murray 1830, Chapter IV 'Taxes on Luxuries'. 'As the effect of these very high duties is in some cases to diminish the revenue, and in all to create smuggling – and further, by greatly diminishing the articles on which they fall, to diminish the demand for, and the exportation of our own manufactures – these duties are exceedingly injurious, and ought to be reduced.' 3rd edition, London: J. Murray, 1831 p. 38.]

be ascertained, with the utmost facility, and no difficulty would present itself, except in fixing a value upon it, a difficulty which might readily be overcome. In point of fact, all that we require concerning it is accomplished imperfectly indeed at present, through the medium of the books of the Bank of England and other joint stock companies, the public taxes and the poor rates.

Circulating property consists of the debts due from one individual to another, of that vast mass of commodities, which are produced, distributed and consumed with more or less rapidity at every movement, and through every part of a civilized country and of what may be considered the capitals of professional men, such as lawyers, physicians etc, their capitals being represented by their annual profit in a way which will be described hereafter.

Debts may be again divided into two classes, the first consisting of mortgages bonds etc, the second of those contracted by commercial men in the common course of their business, and of the debts of private persons with their trades people and with each other.

A registry of the first class might be effected with as much facility as that of fixed property, and would possess the advantage of carrying on its face a valuation of the several items which composed it; such a registry already exists in many countries, and ought to exist in all, where the legislature is desirous of obviating the evils arising from disputes and litigation under our imperfect system of legal procedure.

The next items in the account, consist chiefly of the floating debt due from one person to another, of the circulating medium, and the commodities before alluded to. Now it will be perceived after a little consideration, that these several items (except when they have been exchanged, and pass into the hands of other classes already enumerated, forming then a portion of their income) compose the capitals of the great class of producers, and that, if through any means we can obtain from each of them a knowledge of the value of the capital he employs, or of the profits or income he obtains, we shall have acquired all the information we can desire. To make this more obvious it must be recollected, how easily the wealth of the owners of land and of the unproductive classes who subsist on incomes derived from the public funds, or from sums lent at interest may be ascertained. Taking these away, what class of society remains possessing wealth? Only the commercial and professional class, those who are employed in producing raw produce, in manufacturing commodities from it, in their distribution; or as Lawyers etc. It is obvious then that all the wealth and consequently all the commodities of a country, which do not belong to landowners and to those subsisting on money lent at interest must appertain to the class employed in the various branches of production, and to professional men: thus then having previously shewn that all other property may be easily ascertained, it appears that by obtaining from the class employed in the various branches of commerce and professions an account of its capital and profits, the registration of property may be made universal. Now this difficulty cannot be considered insuperable, for it was wholly or partially overcome, during the existence of the property tax in Great Britain. What has once been effected to a certain extent might be improved and perhaps rendered complete. All that is required for the purpose is to compel the keeping of proper accounts.

But it will be said that the registration itself and the publicity it would occasion would be an overwhelming evil. To this it may be answered that the property of landowners and of some other classes is perfectly open to the observation of all, and no evil consequences are found to arise to them or the community from this circumstance. Still it is objected that great injury and inconvenience would follow to persons engaged in commerce, if their affairs were exposed to a like scrutiny. The very dislike which they express to it is certainly one item of evil which we must take into the account, but we must not forget that all public measures ought to be directed to benefit the greatest number, and especially when the dislike of the minority arises in a considerable degree from a prejudice which reason and experience would remove.

Are all hopes of ever establishing a computable tax to be resigned to please the minority? Does the community derive benefit from allowing to some of its members the power of representing themselves to be richer or poorer than they really are? This point will be considered hereafter.

A remark must here be made once for all, which ought to be kept in mind throughout the whole of the following disquisition. That in weighing the inconveniences attendant upon a tax, other than the loss of its money amount to the payer, or in comparing it with a different impost, we must always consider what sum it produces, is required to produce, or is capable of producing. Thus an amount of evil might be intolerable, and afford at once a ground of rejection to a tax yielding £100,000, which would furnish only a superable objection to one yielding a million, and might be passed over almost unnoticed in an impost yielding ten millions. Thus then in weighing the inconveniences attendant on the excise we must not compare them with one or more petty imposts, but with a whole host, if such can be found, capable of producing say twenty million, and in weighing again the inconveniences of a property tax, we must not compare it with the excise, on the customs, but with all existing imposts in a mass, much as it alone is capable of supplying their place, and rendering them unnecessary.

We may generalize these observations, in the following maxim. The inconveniences attendant on a tax, beyond the money amounts, are to be considered in a direct ratio with the evils inflicted on the Government and payer, and in an inverse ratio with the sum it yields, is capable of yielding, or is required to yield. Thus let the evils produced by a tax on wine be represented by one, and the sum it may produce be two million, and the evils inflicted by a property tax be ten, and the sum it may produce be forty million. The latter would be preferable to the former in the proportion of two to one.

Chapter 5

Simplicity

A tax is called simple which occasions on the part of the Government, the agents, and the payers, the smallest possible number of distinct operations, and those of the easiest performance.

It seems impossible to ascertain at present the maximum of this quality which may be attainable. Experience alone can afford the desired information but there can be no doubt, that existing systems of finance admit of the greatest improvement under the head of simplicity, the importance of which hardly requires elucidation.

It may be sufficient to remark, as has been already done, that the legislature having determined that a certain revenue is necessary, for the purpose of government ought to make its way into the pockets of the subject, by the shortest and easiest route, for by the supposition, that sum being sufficient for the necessities of the State, any unnecessary increase either in the number or difficulty of the operations incident to the tax, is so much useless addition to its amount entailing a sacrifice of happiness on the people, accompanied by no corresponding benefit.

In comparing practically two or more taxes for the purpose of determining which possesses in the highest degree the quality of simplicity, considerable difficulty will sometimes be found in striking a balance, though when the differences are greater, the slightest observation is sufficient to guide the

judgment; the following examples of both kinds of examination, beginning
with the easiest may therefore be useful. What is the relative position in the
scale of simplicity of a polltax which levies the same amount on each individual, an equal duty by tale on commodities imported, a duty ad-valorem
on commodities imported, or an income tax?

Now the only operations in a polltax are: First, a census of the people,
then a visit of the tax gatherer to each individual, each head of a family, or
each responsible chief, or assembly of a district, as the case may be; it will
probably indeed happen that a large proportion of those from whom the tax
is demanded, will be unable to pay it; but that will affect its computability,
constancy &c &c. It will present inconveniences which do not form the subject of the present chapter. Taken in themselves, neither of these operations
presents serious difficulty.

In collecting a duty by tale on commodities imported there are also two
operations:

1. The keeping an account of each separate article;

2. The requiring payment from the owner. But the difficulty in this case is
   much greater than the former. The number of separate articles will be
   larger than the number of population, and ascertained with less ease.

A duty ad-valorem will require three sets of operations:

1. An account to be taken of each separate article;

2. Value to be put upon each;

3. A payment to be obtained from the owner.

The second operation here described will be more difficult because more
liable to error, than any of those described in the two last paragraphs and we

must therefore rank the subject of this after both those which have preceded it, as far as the quality of simplicity is concerned.

The property tax is inferior to all these. The operations it involves as:

1. The discovery of all property and its owners;

2. The putting a value upon it, when it does not consist in money;

3. The demanding the amount of the tax from the persons whom it has finally been determined ought to pay it.

Having gone thus far we must proceed to rectify, and finally fix our judgment, by considering the amount which it is required that the tax should produce. If that amount be very large, it is certain that the duties on imports, owing to the enhancement of price, and consequent smuggling and diminution of consumption, and probable that the polltax, will not furnish sufficient, while by the property tax, we may in case of necessity, without diminishing the national capital, take from each individual all his income, minus the proportion indispensably necessary for his support.

The difficulty of the operations incident to any tax greatly depend on its weight, and the ease of, and temptations to, evasion. Hence arises in a great degree the extreme complexity of indirect taxes in general, the endless laws and regulations of the customs and excise, the necessity of importing, manufacturing or selling goods, of particular sizes, or qualities, at particular places, or times, a system in short so complicated, so unnatural, that perhaps few instances of human ingenuity can be found more surprising, than the comparative ease with which under such shackles, the business of life is carried on. This system in all countries might doubtless be greatly improved, but after Government had done all in its power, an immense mass amount of irremedial evil would still remain.

In reckoning the number of operations involved in the collection of a given tax, and comparing it with any other tax in this respect, it is of little consequence to what number of separate acts, we give the name of an operation, provided we apply the same rule to both, indeed in this respect accuracy can hardly be hoped for, we must choose a mean between the confusion of things dissimilar in their nature, and an overwhelming enumeration of particulars. Among the rules conducive to the establishment of a simple system of taxation, the following may be considered as among the most important.

1. Impose one or two taxes rather than several or many.

2. Two or more taxes of a dissimilar nature are more complex than two or more taxes resembling each other, the latter therefore are so far to be preferred.

Chapter 6

Frugality in Collection

A tax is frugal in collection when it is exacted at small expense, when the power of purchasing previously enjoyed by the people is transferred to the Government with the slightest possible deduction, the perfection of frugality would take place, supposing the power of purchasing could be transferred without any diminution whatever; but as such a degree of perfection is probably unattainable, we must consider this quality to be possessed by a tax, when the loss in transit is reduced to an inconsiderable proportion.

It is unnecessary to insist long upon the utility of reducing to the utmost possible degree the expense of collecting the revenue, when it is considered that the diminution of the national wealth consists in the whole sum taken from the taxpayer, while the advantages derived to the community from this sacrifice on his part, are to be measured only by the net amount, which finally reaches the exchequer, the proportion retained by the tax gatherer being so much totally lost. Prodigal taxes are usually favourites with bad Governments. Hence when we know the rate per cent at which the revenue is collected in different countries we may form an idea, which will be approximately just, as to the relative goodness of their political institutions.

In France the total expense of collection is about fourteen per cent.[1] In

---

[1]See Sir H. Parnell p.114-178 and Marshall's Tables – [Parnell op. cit. chapter ix 'The Collection of the Revenue'; Chapter x 'Bounties and Drawbacks'; chapter xi 'The Management of the Public Expenditure'; J. Marshall *Digest of All the Accounts relating*

England about eight per cent, in Ireland about thirteen per cent. However
we must not forget to modify the inferences from these facts by recollecting,
that the necessary expense of collection will be increased, by the extent of
the territory and thinness of the population, which is to furnish it, by the
imperfection of the means of communication and transmitting money, and
finally by the small total amount of the revenue. Thus the necessary expenses
of collection would be greater in South America, than in the United States,
in the United States than in Italy, in Italy than in France, in France than in
Great Britain.

Let us now lay down a few principles, from which may be drawn the rules
most likely to produce a frugal tax or system of taxation.

1. Other things being equal, that system of revenue will be usually the
   most frugal, which contains the smallest number of separate imposts,
   and consequently if any one tax could be levied, which should, produce
   a sufficient sum to defray the whole expenses of the State, it would
   probably be expedient to adopt it with a view to frugality.

When the exchequer of a Nation is filled from a vast variety of different
sources, it is obvious that the number of officers employed in its exaction
must be proportionably increased; thus in England, some years ago the

---

to the *Population, Productions, Revenues, Financial Operations, Manufactures, Shipping,
Colonies, Commerce, &c. &c. of the United Kingdom of Great Britain and Ireland.* London: printed by J. Haddon, 1833. See Part II p.22 for an account of the costs of collection
of the different heads of revenue of in Great Britain and Ireland. For 1831Marshall gives
the total cost of collection as £3,064,703 for Great Britain, and a folding sheet at the
start of Part II of his compilation, 'Statement III', gives total income for Great Britain
as £50,657,035, resulting in a cost of collection of just over 6 per cent. For Ireland the
situation is more complicated, and it is not clear how Norman arrived at his figure of 13
per cent, though he was skilled in the extraction of data from Marshall's tables, which
were themselves a clever compilation of data from different Parliamentary returns over a
period of 35 years and printed at the instance of the Select Committee on Public Documents of 1833. For 1816, the last year in which separate figures for the British and Irish
Exchequers were provided, the Irish collection costs were £553,456 in the upper part of
the table on p.22 and, under separate headings, £64,876 in the lower part. Total tax
receipts for Ireland are shown on a folding sheet at the start of Part II, 'Statement No 1'
as £7,733,599 giving a collection cost of just under 8 per cent.]

salt duties employed one set of officers, the other internal or excise duties a 2nd, the customs a 3rd and the direct contribution a fourth.

2. Other things being equal, that system of taxation will be most frugal in which the total sum raised, is collected from the smallest number of persons.

   The truth of this principle appears equally manifest with that of the last; because supposing, in order to simplify the question, that we take the sum raised by one tax in a particular district, it is certain that the time of the taxgatherer will be much more fully occupied if he has to collect the required amount from 100 persons than from 10.

3. Other things being equal, a tax will be most frugal, which leaves to the tax payer no other motive of evasion than a wish to avoid the payment of the sum composing it.

It will appear subsequently that many imposts exist, which impose on those who contribute to them, a much greater sacrifice than is represented by the money amount they are required to pay to the State. Now in proportion to the motives to evade a tax must be the means adopted to counteract the effect of these motives.

It follows from what has been said, that with a view to frugality

1. We should endeavour to reduce the number of taxes as much as possible.

2. We should strive to reduce the number of contributors as much as possible.

3. We should never impose through the medium of a tax a greater privation of the power of enjoyment than is represented by the money amount composing it.

These rules deserve to be kept in mind, as their importance is not confined to the quality of frugality; we have already seen, that in a great degree they apply to that of simplicity and their influence will be found to extend very wide, and their violation to be attended with incalculable evil in other respects, besides in increase in the expense of collection. In most countries a great prejudice has existed against the farming of taxes and as it would appear without sufficient reason; at any rate it seems almost demonstrable, that by this mode only, at any given time, the greatest degree of frugality could be attained. Even the best Government that has ever existed is less interested in reducing the expenses of collection than a private individual would be, and in most countries the motives of the ruling powers operate in an opposite direction. Supposing the interest and intelligence of both were upon an equality, all that the former could gain by collecting the revenue through its own agents would be to save the profits of the latter, which would be reduced to a minimum through the means of open competition; the question therefore is whether the more direct interest of the contractor would not produce a saving in expense, more than equal to the profit he would gain by the operation?

Should it be said in reply to these observations that in many countries, as Spain for instance, the revenue when farmed was found to fall very short of what it yielded when collected immediately, by the agents of Government, and that the avarice, cruelty and luxury of the Fermiers generaux, caused their very name to be regarded with abhorrence in France before the revolution, the observation might be answered by pointing out that under despotic Governments there is no publicity, no justice, and that in the instances above stated, where the taxes were based in ignorance and oppression, and their produce scandalously misapplied, the rulers were eager to augment the unpopularity of a class of useful public servants, in order to diminish their own. Thus Sismondi[2] observes that in Italy the Governments that arose after the

---

[2]Sismondi Histre des Repub. Italiennes chapr 27 Vol. 16, p. 435. [J. Simonde de

foreign invasions in the 16th century, participated at length so far in the prejudices of their subjects, as to declare the officers of justice infamous; the oppression exercised in the name of the law, excited a general dislike against those who were charged with putting it in execution, and the ruling powers were too happy in the opportunity of shifting from their own shoulders a portion of that public indignation, which so properly belonged to their crimes.

To farm all the revenues of a great and highly taxed Nation might be a burden too heavy for any one man, or even for any one company, but at any rate it might be adopted to a greater extent than at present with regard to particular taxes.

Sismondi *Histoire des Republiques Italiennes du Moyen Age* 5th edition, Brussels, 1839, vol. viii, p. 505. On Norman's purchase of this work see his *Autobiography*. While convalescing at Ramsgate in 1816, Norman purchased the first '9 or 10' volumes of the Sismondi work. Given the publishing history of this work, this suggests that he had purchased part of the first edition. Vols 1-4 were published by H. Gessner in Zurich, Vols 5-8 by Nicholls in Paris, and Vols. 9-15 by Treuttel and Würtz in Paris, extending over the years 1807-15. Given Norman's imprecision about exactly how many volumes he initially purchased, and the fact that he later completed the set to include the volume to which he refers, it seems possible that he purchased the final volumes from a later edition, such as the Paris 1809-18 or Paris 1826 editions, published by Treuttel and Würtz.]

Chapter 7

Constancy

A tax is constant, when its produce is certain as to amount and time of receipt, and not likely to vary from the dictates of fashion, caprice or avarice, from the variations of seasons, and from political circumstances.

So little difference of opinion can exist upon the propriety, nay in a certain degree upon the necessity, of a tax possessing this quality, that it will not detain us long. All must allow that Nation might suffer the greatest inconvenience, or even be exposed to the most imminent danger, in case the funds which had been calculated upon to supply the wants of the Government were suddenly to fail in the very hour of need; ammunition could not be purchased, the pay of armies would fall into arrears and there would be a necessity for having recourse to forced requisitions, to contributions, and to all that species of irregular exaction, by which for the safety of the whole Nation, a heavy privation is inflicted upon one portion of it. In such a case the sacrifice must be made, but nobody can deny that it is highly desirable to obviate the necessity of exacting it.

The disadvantages resulting from a tax, which produces to the exchequer more than is expected from it, are not so obvious as those of a tax which yields less than was anticipated, they are however sufficiently palpable. In calculating the expenses necessary for the welfare of the State, the legislature places in the hands of the executive, what it considers sufficient to meet them. If these funds yield a larger sum than was expected, if follows, that an unnecessary burden has been imposed on the people; for it must never be forgotten, that the best imaginable tax, must deprive them of enjoyments, or of the power of enjoying, equal to what might be purchased by the net produce of the tax added to the expense of collection.

But it may be said that no inconvenience will result from an excess of revenue in one year, because that excess may defray the expenses of the succeeding year. To this the answer is that the direct interest of all Governments is to spend as much as they can, and that, if they are furnished in any given year with more than the necessary means, the consequence, at the very best will be a want of that rigid parsimony which is so desirable, in order that the expenditure may be reduced to its lowest term, while in ordinary circumstances a wide door will be opened to jobbing and speculation.

However much the revenue might have exceeded the estimate, we should seldom find, that means had not been found to dissipate it; even granting that the surplus had been saved and was ready to diminish the taxation necessary for the ensuing year, it might happen that many of the contributors, owing to peculiar circumstances, would by no means be recompensed by this diminution, or in other words, that an unnecessary evil had been inflicted on them.

Chapter 8

Divisibility

A tax is divisible which admits of easy and gradual increase and diminution from the smallest to the largest amount.

The power of being augmented and lessened as may be required is evidently a property of great importance. Unless a tax or a system of taxation possesses this property, it will be impossible to adapt the revenue exactly to the ever varying state of the country; one while profoundly tranquil, the next week or month, threatened with internal commotions or foreign hostilities, and a short time afterwards, on the point of being overwhelmed by a superior power to resist which, its fiscal resources must be stretched to the utmost possible degree. Not a long period may elapse before the storm disappears, and it becomes expedient to reduce without delay the expenditure to that point whence it had been so suddenly raised. Now it cannot be denied that under all such sudden alterations, it would be desirable that the legislature should have the power of adapting the revenue exactly to the demands upon it; that it should be able suddenly and largely to increase it, when great pecuniary means were necessary; that it should be able to reduce its amount, without delay, when this necessity had ceased, so that on one hand, the state might not be exposed to danger, while on the other, the sacrifices of the people might cease with the circumstances requiring them.

Owing to the comprehensive nature of the quality of computability it may appear that those of constancy, and divisibility, especially the former are included under it. Certain it is that they are usually united, especially the two first. Still as they present very different ideas to the mind, it is most convenient to separate them. Constancy and divisibility generally go together, but there are taxes, which while continued at a certain rate, will yield with considerable certainty the expected produce, but which if either augmented or diminished, will baffle the calculations of the expertest financier.

It may be farther observed with regard to the qualities of computability, constancy, and divisibility, that unless a financial system possesses them, the Government whenever it passes laws, either to increase or diminish the revenue, will legislate in the dark, it will not produce the intended effect at all, or it will produce more or less than the intended effect. In any of these cases, great inconvenience or even danger may be the result. Chance will occupy the place of reason, and the interest of millions of rational beings will be decided by the principle which presides over the rattle of a dice box, or the whirls of a teetotum.[1]

---

[1] [A teetotum is a four-sided top with sides lettered to determine gain or loss of the spinner.]

Chapter 9

Popularity

A tax is called popular when it excites no unnecessary degree of alarm or dislike.

The perfection of popularity would be obtained if the tax in all the various processes preceding and attendant upon its collection excited no other painful sensations, among the various individuals composing the community than the loss of the enjoyments which its money amount plus the smallest expense of collection, could procure them.

The propriety of attending to these circumstances, may be shewn in a variety of ways, in the first place, alarm and dislike are disagreeable feelings, they are positive pain, and diminish the mass of happiness; the legislator therefore, who ought ever to aim at producing the greatest amount of good, with the least drawback of evil, is bound to reduce them to their lowest term. In some cases such as that of taxes falling on wages, the degree of odium excited is excessive and unmerited, after the impost has been some time in operation. The government ought then in the first place to take every possible means of enlightening the public mind. Such a line of conduct cannot fail to produce a considerable effect, for even the lowest and most ignorant of the people, are quicksighted to discover their real interest, when the means of arriving at the truth are placed fairly before them. Should however this method wholly fail of success which may happen, it will then become the duty of the sovereign to calculate calmly, whether it be not possible to substitute something else in lieu of the obnoxious tax, and in forming this calculation, the advantages in other respects being equal, or nearly equal, superior popularity ought to turn the scale.

To prevent then a diminution of public happiness from the direct excitement of painful feelings is one strong reason for the selection of popular taxes, another not less so is, that a popular tax is usually collected at small expense, because the contributors have in general no very strong wish to evade it, and because if they had, the overwhelming influence of public opinion, would add an irresistible force to the terrors of the law. An unpopular tax always affords increased facilities to the smuggler, because it enlists the sympathies of the public in his favour; thus a part of the numerous evils which follow attempts either successful or not to evade the revenue laws, fall under this head.

The amount of taxation on the whole, and the objects to which it is applied, though not falling within the scope of this work affect in a great degree its popularity. A fiscal system will never excite a very violent feeling of dislike, when the persons and property of the subject are secured in the most complete manner, and at a moderate expense.

It can hardly be doubted but that if this maxim were rigidly observed, the popular voice might be directed with the most powerful effect against those persons who attempted to evade the payment of the public dues, and that few would be found so thoroughly abandoned, as to endeavour to escape contributing their fair proportion to an order of things from which they derived such immense advantages. What would be thought of a man who was known to cheat his baker and his butcher deliberately and upon system? May it not be supposed that a Government, of which the excellencies were palpable and indisputable, might equally seek refuge from those who attempted to elude its just demands, under the impenetrable aegis of public opinion.

It is said that at Hamburgh, a portion of the public expenses was once paid by a general tax, to which it was understood that each person should contribute according to his means. The exact amount he was to pay was not prescribed to him, he put what he thought proper into a box, which was not opened until all had paid their shares, so that the amount contributed by every particular person could never be known but to himself, and yet it is said that attempts at evasion rarely occurred. It must not be forgotten that the public expenses at Hamburg were extremely small, and from this and other instances we may safely conclude that an exercise of the most rigid parsimony, a reduction of all unnecessary expenses will be one sure means of making taxation popular.

Chapter 10

Noninterference

A tax is called noninterferent when it leaves the national industry to flow into those channels which it would occupy naturally, did not tax exist and when it opposes no obstacles to the processes by which commodities would be produced and distributed without it.

Had this essay been published half a century ago, it would have been necessary to have written a volume to prove the truth of the propositions involved in this definition of noninterference; happily at the present day juster notions of economical science prevail than then existed. However difficult it may be to procure the repeal or modification of laws which proceed from opposite principles, few will be found bold enough to deny their abstract truth. Even now however when protecting duties find no advocator, except among those who think them serviceable to their individual interests, and the profound reasoners who conceive every absurdity sacred, if it has been only acted upon for 500 or even 100 years; it may not be useless to state the simple principles on which the propriety of leaving industry unfettered is founded.

Every individual or the great mass of individuals know better how to employ their capital and labor beneficially than the government can do. From this it follows that if left to themselves, the majority will so employ them, and as the wealth and happiness of the community is formed of the aggregate

riches and enjoyments of all its members, to allow them to turn their industry
to whatever objects they think fit, must be the surest means of increasing its
productive powers.

But in order, more clearly to point out the bad consequences, that flow
from the introduction of the opposite principles, let us trace out their effects
in the following short and simple example of what is called a protecting duty.

Suppose that owing to a congenial climate, or to the superiority of skill in
her manufacturers, France can produce silken goods of a better quality and at
a cheaper rate than England and that in consequence under the operation of
a free system of commercial intercourse, the former country exports annually
to the latter 1000 yards of silk which cost 3s per yard, or £150 in all. It
is obvious that for this sum the inhabitants of Great Britain are provided
with an useful and beautiful commodity and that they cannot be benefited,
except by obtaining it [at] a reduced price, or of a still better quality, but
their rulers are of a different opinion; they wish, as it is called, to assist the
national industry, to stimulate the growth of silk manufacture at home, and
at the same time to increase the revenue. With these views they impose a
duty on french silk of 3s per yard, and after much capital has been fruitlessly
wasted in abortive speculation, and the trade becomes once more fixed on a
stable footing, it is found that the legislature has partly gained its objects;
1000 yards of silk still compose the annual consumption, and of these 500
are produced at home; but as the advantages of climate, and perhaps of
skill, continue on the side of France, the price at which the 500 yards can be
sold, so as to remunerate the manufacturers, amounts to 5s per yard. The
remaining 500 yards are still imported, and pay the duty to Government, so
that they now cost the consumer 6s per yard.

Let us now observe the effects of the supposed protecting duty on the
wealth, and consequently on the enjoyment, or the power of enjoyment of
the community. Before the imposition of the tax, the account stood thus.

But this £50 is not the only loss to be sustained by Great Britain. There

1000 yards of French Silk at 3s per yard	£150
Afterwards 500 yards French Silk at 6s per yard - £150	
plus 500 yards English Silk at 5s per yard - £125	£275
[Loss]	£125
Deduct duty on 500 yards at 3s per yard	£75
Absolute loss to the country so far	£50

is the expense of collection, and of the prevention of smuggling, which last charge must be considerable, when the temptation is so great as the difference between 6s and 3s or 50 per cent. Then comes the demoralization, which follows an habitual disregard of the laws, and other evils which will be particularized hereafter. Last of all comes an evil, which in the example above cited is not so palpable as in others which might have been adduced, but which even then appears of considerable moment, vis the difference in quality between the silk consumed before and after the imposition of the protecting duty. In the latter case 500 yards of french silk is consumed at the high price of 6s per yard while British may be had for 5s which is as much as to say, that, in the opinion of the consumer, it is superior in quality by at least 1s to its competitor; its superiority cannot be less, but may be greater, for we have no evidence that it would not still continue to be consumed, even did it cost 7s or 8s a yard; but taking that view of the case most favourable for the framers of the duty, we see that it compels the community to consume 500 yards of Silk, which is worth at the least 1s a yard less than another description of silk, which it might consume, did no tax exist, or was the tax imposed in such a way as not to interfere with the natural distribution of capital and industry. This £25 being added to the former amount of loss; it appears that the community is put to an increased expense of £150, besides charges of collection, of gaols to hold smugglers and of lawyers to prosecute them, of which £75 only, ever finds its way into the exchequer. The remainder is absolutely lost, and lost more perniciously to the State, than if a quantity of commodities of the same value, had been thrown into the sea, or consumed in a bonfire on the 5th of November; for then no new incentives to immorality would have been created.

It is not meant to be asserted that the actual state of the silk trade in Great Britain before the late change was such as the above example would seem to represent. On the contrary, most unprejudiced men were then persuaded that owing to the great advantages we possessed in capital and machinery, we might set all foreign competition at defiance, as soon as the enormous duty on the raw material was lowered in a reasonable proportion, and the skill of the manufacturer stimulated by competition. Experience has shown that they were right. Nevertheless the example given will still be an exact portrait of the whole class of protecting duties, for it must always be recollected, that if every one of them does not produce the consequences therein described, it has no effect whatever, it is a mere dead letter, retained only to fill up the vacant pages of the statute book. If protecting duties have any effect at all they must as such, act in the way we have seen.

It may be said, in order to cancel the last item in the account of loss, that the English silk is really as good as the French, and that it is only the influence of caprice or fashion, or the innate perversity of human nature, which induces our country-men to pay willingly a higher price for the latter, than the former; to all this it can only be replied, that every individual is the best judge of his own interest, and that he who prefers Dannemora to Staffordshire iron, the wine of champagne to that of the cape, venison to pork, and turtle to calves-head, does so on exactly the same principle as he who buys french instead of English silk; both may be deceived, but we cannot guard against such mistakes, the people are incomparably less likely to be deceived than the Government; and at any rate as we have no better, and indeed no other rule to judge by, than the common opinion of the public, we must consider its award as final, and form our calculations upon it.

It may further be observed that a protecting duty affords no advantage whatever, even to the manufacturers of the favored article, except when owing to some peculiar circumstances, it prevents the competition of other capitalists in the same country, and establishes a close monopoly in their favor. In general they can only obtain the common rate of profit, and this common rate cannot possibly be raised by a protecting duty, but must on the contrary be lowered, first by that part of it which falls directly on profits, secondly by that part of it which falls on them indirectly through the medium of wages, in the case of an impost on necessaries; for ceteris paribus, wages rise eventually whenever the price of an article in general use among laborers is augmented; as would be the case with a commodity exposed to a protecting duty, or created by the stimulus thus afforded, and which would of course be dearer and worse than what previously supplied its place.

A few simple rules will enable us to estimate with sufficient exactness the loss sustained by a Nation from the operation of a protecting duty, whenever we can arrive at a knowledge of the data necessary to form the calculation, these data are:

1. The price of the commodity which has been, or would be consumed, under a system of free trade.

2. The quantity of it, that has been, or would be consumed.

3. The price of the favored commodity.

4. The total quantities of both consumed after the introduction of the tax, and the proportion they bear to each other.

5. The net amount of duty paid into the exchequer.

It would be desirable to add to these an account of the expense of collection, and of the increased stimulus given to crime, as evinced in the augmented charges of arresting and prosecuting offenders, nor must we wholly forget the miseries of these unhappy beings, whom the acts of their rulers have needlessly allured into the path of error. In the case of a new protecting duty we must farther also consider the losses which necessarily arise whenever trade is suddenly forced to seek new channels, before capital and labour are again duely distributed. This miscellaneous mass of evil cannot be reduced to an exact pecuniary calculation; it will be however sufficient, if we represent it in our minds as an indefinite though, weighty addition to the calculated loss which shall appear to have been inflicted by the protecting duty, upon an estimate formed upon the preceding data.

The rules for forming the calculation are:

1. To deduct the cost of the commodities which had been consumed or would be consumed, under a system of free trade, from that of those consumed after the imposition of the duty. The difference will be the additional cost to the consumer.

2. To multiply the proportional difference in price between the favored and obnoxious commodity by the quantity of the former; consumed after the imposition of the tax and to add the produce to the sum resulting from the application of the first rule.

3. To deduct from the final balance the net sum paid into the exchequer.

Many taxes are interferent although not intended to favor the consumption of one commodity rather than another, owing to the obstacles they oppose to the best mode of production or transport. The imposts on malt and glass in England are instances of this evil; and almost the whole class of indirect taxes sin in the same way, though less palpably.

Prohibitions produce the same effects, in kind as protecting duties, but the former have the bad effects of the worst duty, without yielding anything to the exchequer.

Bounties resemble protecting duties in being interferent, though they operate in a different way. Their direct effect is to favor the consumption of some particular commodity by enabling purchasers to obtain it at a price less than the costs of production. While protecting duties aim at the same end by raising the cost of production of an article which in the natural state of things would supersede that which the legislator wishes to favor, when paid upon articles usually exported, they become a tribute to foreigners. Reason and sound policy can never justify them, except as temporary expedients, under certain rare, and extraordinary contingencies.

It must be observed however that the name of a bounty is sometimes given to what is really a drawback, the repayment of a tax previously paid and intended to remove the interference occasioned by it. No system of indirect taxes can be other than interferent, which is not accompanied by a well regulated scale of drawbacks, yet it must be remarked that the advantage hereby obtained, is almost limited to foreign trade, that the existence of drawbacks is replete with the danger of frauds on the revenue, and the certainty of heavy expense, and that in many cases, as where a duty is levied on an article of raw produce, and the drawback repaid on the same article in a manufactured state it is almost impossible to fix the latter at a proper amount; it will almost invariably be either too low or too high, becoming in the latter case a bounty as has happened with the drawback on refined sugar in this country which gives a premium to the colonial planter of above 5s–/per Cwt, and therefore costs the consumers from £800,000 to a million per annum. Even when a drawback on a manufactured article has been once fixed at a proper amount, this advantage can never be long retained owing to the constant changes and improvements in the process of fabrication.

On the whole it may be doubted whether drawbacks all things considered, in their present state, do not produce more evil than they remove, while their usual applicability to foreign trade alone, and the extreme difficulty if not impossibility of adjusting them properly, afford one, among many arguments, against all schemes of indirect taxation.[1]

---

[1] For some good observations on Drawbacks see Sir H. Parnell on Fin. Reform p.124.

Sir H. P. erroneously limits the loss arising from the Drawbacks on refined Sugar to the amount exported – forgetting that its effect is to raise the price of all sugar consumed at home. [Parnell op. cit. chapter x 'Bounties and Drawbacks'. Parnell was however concerned that the drawbacks acted as bounties on production, allowing the producers to enjoy increased returns as technology increased with output.]

Chapter 11

Equality

A tax is called equal when it takes from each person possessing wealth an exactly similar proportion of his property.

The perfection of equality would exist if the enjoyments of each person possessing property, *after the payment of the tax should bear the same relation in respect of his property* to those of other persons which they did before the tax was imposed, in other words, if the sacrifices imposed were exactly equal.

Equality of taxation is favorable to the aggregate of human happiness from its tendency to save the pain arising from the seeing a preference given without any special ground to another. If I am exempted from a tax, without any strong reason being assigned, peculiarly warranting the exemption, a painful sensation is created in the rest of the community at beholding the superior privilege conferred upon me. It is true that I have the pleasure of being preferred, but I am one, and they are many, the pleasure is confined to one bosom the pain extends to hundreds.

The chief objects of this chapter will be to show that:

1. The aim of a Government when it imposes a tax, should be to conform as nearly as possible to the second proposition at the head of this chapter.

2. That the first contains the best practical rule for so doing. The proof

in both cases presents greater difficulties than are usually found in the discussion of fiscal questions, and will require more than a common share of the reader's attention. It is sufficiently obvious however that the perfection here held up to the legislators' view, can never be fully attained; even supposing such a state of society as the laws of Lycurgus attempted to establish at Sparta, a perfect equality of wealth among all the members of the community.[1] Let us imagine a Nation wherein each individual should be worth £100 and should be called upon to contribute £5 annually to the public service. Even here the necessary conditions would not be fulfilled. A – from ill health, from taste, or from some other cause would desire more expensive pleasures than B. C's great enjoyment would be to amass while D would have no wish to accumulate. In this case it is plain, that the payment of the tax would make a greater inroad into the felicity of A and C than on that of B and D, nor would it be in the power of the legislator to correct this evil with any degree of certainty, because he could never tell before hand the exact degree in which each of his subjects would be driven to adopt some rule or other and that of a tax of a similar amount on each would doubtless appear to him the best that could be devised as a similarity of disposition characterizes the majority.

But it may be asked even though the sovereign could so exactly apportion his tax, by varying the sum levied on each contributor, as to leave the enjoyments of each after it was paid in the same relation to those of all others, as they stood in before it was imposed, would it be desirable that he should so vary them. We answer, yes, because in that case the maximum of felicity

---

[1] [Lycurgus, by tradition the law giver of Sparta, though there is doubt whether such a person, as distinct from a cult, ever existed. Norman appears to be alluding to the attribution to Lycurgus (or Lykurgus) of a policy of equal distribution of land, an attribution which his friend George Grote explicitly rejected in his twelve volume history of Greece (1846). The origin of the story appears to lie in a biography of Lycurgus by Plutarch, though he in turn may have taken it from earlier sources. See G. Grote *History of Greece*, Vol. II. Second edition, London: J. Murray, 1849, pp. 512, 530-560, especially p. 534.]

on the whole would be attained, and the revenue necessary for the State would be raised with the smallest possible loss of happiness. The apparent injustice arising from the difference in the money payment, would disappear in the real equality of the sacrifice by which the advantages of Government were purchased. The enjoyments of a man as far as they can be affected by his wealth, are in an inverse proportion to his wants and a direct proportion to his means of gratifying them; supposing the former to be placed beyond our control, our only means of preserving an approach to equality will be by varying the latter which are within our grasp.

It appears then that in a community where wealth was equally distributed, a perfectly wise and benevolent legislature would require the same sum from each person, and it necessarily follows, that where wealth is unequally distributed, those whose fortunes are equal should contribute an equal sum to the exchequer, but a question of considerable difficulty now presents itself. Should the proportion of tax be the same at every point in the scale of property, should A, the man worth £100, pay £5 while B, the man worth £100,000, paid only £5000. With considerable diffidence, in opposition perhaps to the common opinion, and to the practice of some legislatures, we answer that he should. If any other rule could be laid down which would insure a greater equality of sacrifice such a rule ought to be adopted, but none presents itself on which full reliance could be placed. In the case supposed, such is the difference in the wants that prevail in the several classes of society that A might possibly suffer no more from the deduction of five per cent from his fortune than B; he might even suffer less. Let us suppose only 50 per cent of all his pleasurable sensations were derived from his wealth, while that of B furnished 80 per cent of his, the happiness of the former would be diminished after payment of the tax only two and a half per cent, that of the latter four per cent.

This illustration may appear trifling, but the subject is so important that nothing which can throw light on it ought to be disregarded. Again, it may be asked if the public happiness would not be promoted by taking £10,000 from B and exempting 2000 A's from any tax what so ever? One objection to this plan if acted upon to a great extent would be that it would operate as a tax upon accumulation, a tax on prudence, on that habit, which it is so essential should be cherished. But the overwhelming objection would be the general insecurity that would flow from it. The rule that each person possessing wealth should contribute an equal proportion of it to the exigencies of the State, is clear and precise, and when abandoned leaves no sure and stable basis on which to fix the public burthens.[2] If this be given up no other presents itself which it is so much the interest of the greater number to adopt. Should an individual or class, endeavour to make those, richer than themselves, pay in a greater ratio than that of their greater wealth, they at once lay themselves open to the classes below them, and expose their own fortunes to a similar attack; the motive arising from this consideration extends even to the lowest class of labourers, who with a vast superiority of physical power, are not likely to see unmoved, the example set them by their superiors. It may be useful to state this argument at greater length.

Let us suppose that the community are considering what sum they shall take from A, they may either tax him proportionably to his wealth compared with what they take from B or C or D; or they may take from him more or less. It will not be their interest to take from him less, because then they must make up the deficit among themselves; neither will it be their interest to take from him more, for then neither B, C or D can possibly be secure that it will not come to their turn next to be taxed in a ratio greater than

---

[2][On the question of progression amongst Norman's contemporaries see D.P. O'Brien, *The Classical Economists Revisited*. Princeton: Princeton University Press, 2004 pp. 301-3, 392 notes 91 and 97. Norman's view agrees with that of J.R. McCulloch in his *A Treatise on the Principles and Practical Influence of Taxation and the Funding System* (1845) ed. D.P. O'Brien, Edinburgh: Scottish Academic Press, 1975 pp. 145-147. 'The moment you abandon, in the framing of such taxes, the cardinal principle of exacting from all individuals the same proportion of their income or their property, you are at sea without rudder or compass, and there is no amount of injustice or folly you may not commit.' *Ibid.* p. 147.]

their wealth; In order to obtain security that they themselves shall not be taxed in this larger and indefinite proportion, they purchase the vote of A, in favor of equality, by voting for an impost no more than equal upon him. There is no other possible mode in which they can obtain security or feel that an indefinite amount of enjoyment may not be abstracted from themselves, and thus it will be the interest of B, C and D and all the rest to advocate a system of taxation which abstracts an equal proportion from the wealth of each, and as a necessary branch of this, to vote for taking no more from A than such a system prescribes.

It may be farther remarked that little gain would accrue to the mass of taxpayers from any extra burdens thrown on the wealthy. Persons possessing great riches are few in number, and their property bears but a small proportion to the aggregate riches of the community.

If after all taxation, bearing the same ratio to wealth at every point of the scale, should press in a somewhat heavier degree on the poorer classes than on the very rich, which however is by no means apparent, there seems to be no remedy for the evil which would not introduce still greater evils in its train. A limit however might be fixed below which the sum that each person could justly be called upon to pay would be so small, and the consequent costs of collection so heavy, that from that consideration, the exactions of the taxgatherer should cease. Experience alone can show, where this limit is to be found.

The doctrine of equality of sacrifice, by which it has been shown, that the interest of those possessing wealth, would be best consulted through the means of taxation assessed in the same proportion upon the fortunes of all, leads to the important conclusion, that no attempt should ever be made to tax the laborer, who possesses no other property except his clothes, perhaps a little furniture, and the instruments of his toil, by abstracting however small a portion of his wages, which in all old countries furnish him even when entire, with far less of the necessaries and enjoyments of life than the benevolent observer would desire he should possess. Fortune he has none, his person indeed can be made useful to the State, and he must be prepared to employ it in the public service, when the general good demands such a sacrifice on his part, but then the superior classes ought to be equally called upon to devote *their* persons when required. What is here objected to, is the exaction from the laborer of:

1. A portion of his wages as an equivalent to that tax on their property, which his superiors pay.

2. His personal service along with theirs as soon as the labourer has accumulated sufficient to purchase his cottage, or place a small sum on interest, he becomes pro tanto a proprietor, and must take his change with his new colleagues.

As the wages of labour in all old countries are so low, as hardly to allow the laborer to subsist, and continue his race, all imposts which fall upon the whole class such as a capitation tax, or a duty upon articles of general consumption, end by raising wages to their full amount, and thus diminish profits; but a considerable interval may elapse under certain circumstances, before this effect is produced, during which time the tax is cruelly unequal, and occasions a large mass of suffering to the lower orders.

Those laborers alone can afford to pay taxes, who are unmarried, or have no children, and thus are enabled to expend on themselves the amount of wages, which is calculated to support a man with a family of a medium size; persons so circumstanced pay considerably to the English exchequer, from their extra consumption of beer, spirits, tobacco and other exciseable articles.

In the next section it will be seen that a large majority of all existing imposts are unequal. They are not particularized here, in order to avoid repetitions.

Chapter 12

Uncorruptiveness

A tax may be called uncorruptive which affords the slightest incentive to vice and crimes, and which involves the least inducement or necessity to abstain from useful and agreeable, and to commit pernicious and painful, actions. The term corruptive is applied to those taxes which by the excitement of injurious motives obstruct directly virtues produced by agreeable actions in the same way as the interferent taxes obstruct the process of production and distribution. Both affect the public happiness in a secondary way, the first more immediately, the second through the medium of wealth.

The perfection of uncorruptiveness would be attained, if a tax should in no ways influence the actions of any persons, but those who really paid it, and if its effects upon the latter, were limited to those resulting from the simple disbursements of its money amount.

It is unnecessary to enforce those arguments which must necessarily present themselves to the reader's mind in favor of an incorruptive taxation and it will only therefore be desirable to make a few cursory observations on the best means of securing it. In doing this, it is expedient to consider the two members of the definition separately, taking first those cases in which happiness is affected through the medium of what is called morality. And secondly all other cases.

Under the first head:

The following are rules, the adoption of which would greatly conduce to prevent mischief to the public morals through the medium of taxation:

1. Take care that the whole temptations to evade the tax be merely to escape the payment of the money amount which composes it. In this point of view the quality of uncorruptiveness is nearly coextensive with that of frugality and non-interference.

2. Diminish the number of those who are to pay the tax, as much as is consistent with equality, and contrive that no other persons shall be able to gain by evading it.

3. Hold out no temptation to crimes and vices for the purpose of subsequently raising a revenue from them.

4. Take care generally that taxes be levied in such a way, as not to weaken the regard for truth and the other moralities on which the virtue of the community so much depends.

5. Never impose a tax on the performance of an useful action, so as to afford a motive for the non-performance of the action with a view of escaping from the impost.

The first of these rules is disregarded by the framers of all restrictive and prohibitive duties, of all regulations which interfere with the free development of capital and industry. Those who will please to recollect the illustration given under the head of noninterference, in which it appears that a tax is inflicted on the community equal to £150 while the revenue received by the exchequer is only £50 must instantly perceive, that the temptation to evade the tax, and consequently to break the Laws and violate oaths, is equal to the former amount, while the benefit accruing is to be measured by the latter, the difference being so much devoted, if we may use the expression to bribe the people into the commission of crime, without any corresponding advantage whatever.[1] It is true that some commodities can hardly from their nature be smuggled, and if so, the duties on them, however interferent, are not corruptive. That on timber is an instance.[2]

Suppose a district in which there reside two receivers of rent ten capitalists and 100 laborers. We have already seen that rent and profits are the only two proper objects of taxation at any time, almost the only sources from which revenue can ever ultimately be drawn. A wise legislator therefore in the case under consideration would raise all the money he required by a direct tax on the twelve individuals above-mentioned; if instead of this he was to adopt customs or an excise, he would either expose the whole community, or a great proportion of it to the temptation of breaking the laws, violating oaths &c; by the first line of conduct this evil would extend to only twelve persons, by the second to 100 while under the most favorable supposition it could possess no advantage whatever in the other respects.

The mode of raising revenue by a lottery or by taxing gambling houses, is a most flagrant violation of the third rule. If indeed it could be shown that a certain quantum of vice must exist, a tax upon it might be uncorruptive, supposing that it was accompanied by nothing calculated to increase this quantum, but in the instance above referred to, how contrary is this assumption to the fact, and how certainly do those Governments who protect and encourage gambling houses, create an enormous mass of misery, which would never have existed, had it not been for their interference, and this for the purpose of raising a sum of money which in a national point of view is small and precarious. A tax levied on murderers would not differ from them in principle but only [in] degree, supposing it formed by persons whose interest induced them to augment the frequency of assassination. This point will be

---

[1] [Norman was taken to Hastings for an extended stay to convalesce in 1804, and the Norman family had been regular visitors there from 1801. He observed that the economy of the town depended on fishing, smuggling and gambling, the smuggling being conducted quite openly and with the approval of the townspeople.]

[2] [Norman was for many years a timber merchant. See below p. 86.]

more particularly examined hereafter.

France affords the most flagrant instance of the violation of the third rule, calculated to make taxation incorruptive. The system once pursued in England affords unfortunately the most palpable example of the infraction of the fourth.

If a conspiracy had been formed against the national integrity, with the deliberate purpose of producing a sovereign contempt for truth itself, could those concerned in it have hit upon a plan more adapted to further their nefarious designs, than those numberless official oaths which are required in all transactions with our custom house and excise. They are multiplied as if with an intention of bringing them into contempt, in some instances they are demanded of a man, who cannot possibly know whether the fact to which he deposes be true or not, in others, perhaps when he and all who hear him know, that he swears falsely, and in all they are administered with a degree of haste and disregard to common decency equally offensive and injurious.

Religion is specially interested in the correction of this crying evil.

The class of offences committed by fiscal legislators under the second head of the definition of corruptiveness against the happiness of mankind, contains an appalling list which will be particularly examined in the next section. The most important items in it consist of the taxes on justice, on knowledge, and on the conveyance of intelligence, on health &c &c.

One general remark occurs in almost all the cases of corruptive taxation; their worst effect is produced when they are not in reality paid at all, when they act as a penalty, and thus deter from the performance of a useful action, when once paid, they usually become unequal, and fall naturally under that head. This is a peculiarity which deserves constantly to be borne in mind; in most instances, imposts are only, or most corruptive, when they are wholly unproductive. A tax may be thus conceived which in no case what so ever would produce a shilling, but which would prevent a prodigious mass of human happiness.

One simple maxim would at once remove all the imposts here animadverted on; let none be enacted which either directly or indirectly interfere with the actions of men, or which gives them any motive to behave after the tax has been imposed differently from what they would have otherwise done. This seems to follow naturally from the all important proposition that individuals are better judges of what is most conducive to their happiness than a Government, and that the only effort of the latter should be, to prevent each man from injuring another, by the imposition of specific penalties; we shall subsequently enquire if this rule should be ever deviated from, in our examination of taxes, which are supposed to have a good moral effect, such as those on spirituous liquors. If these have really such an effect, they are of course so far incorruptive in a very high degree.

Chapter 13

Unvexatiousness

A tax is unvexatious which occasions the slightest possible annoyance, trouble loss of time or money to the individuals paying it, in consequence of its nature and of the manner in which it is assessed and collected.

The perfection of this quality would be obtained, if all the inconveniences attending the payment of a tax could be reduced to the disbursement of a sum, at a particular place and time, known beforehand, in apportioning which it would be unnecessary to arm the officers of Government with inquisitorial powers of any kind.

Great difficulty has been encountered in the choice of a fitting name for the quality above defined, and this difficulty has not been thoroughly overcome. The term chosen is uncommon, and wanting in euphony, but it was necessary to choose between it, and the introduction of a completely new word from the learned languages, which would have involved the author in a charge of affectation. It were much to be wished, that a greater licence should be allowed in this respect, especially to those who are treating of a subject comparatively new, for there must always be danger, at least of a want of precision when a word, loaded with old associations, is employed in a novel or unusual sense.

The importance of the quality now under consideration is great; a tax which possesses it may produce £1000 and yet occasion a less sacrifice of public happiness than another producing only £500 and this wholly owing to the annoyance to the payer attending the collection of the latter. These inconveniences may be principally arranged under the following heads.

1. The mode in which a tax is levied may render it necessary that the whole pecuniary circumstances of the tax-payer should be made public. Such is the effect of a property tax.

2. The mode in which a tax is levied may occasion a necessity for the frequent presence and inspection of the agents of Government. Such is the effect of excise or assessed taxes like those of England.

3. The tax-payer may be compelled to make an extra sacrifice of time or money, in order to discharge his share of the tax in the manner prescribed by the law. Such was the effect of the tax paid by the Jews to the Romans at the time of our Saviour's birth, when each contributor was obliged to repair to the place to which his family belonged.

4. The tax-payer may be called upon to pay his tax, at uncertain and inconvenient periods. Such is the Case with the Law taxes in England.

5. The tax may be required in a multiplicity of small sums, each of which perhaps occupies as much time to discharge them, as would be required for the whole, could it be received at once. This is an inconvenience more remarkable in financial systems, than in individual taxes. No country suffers more from it than England.

6. In order to ascertain the exact number and description of the objects liable to the tax, minute returns may be required, and mistakes, punishable by the law, become sometimes unavoidable. The assessed taxes in England afford an example.

Other inconveniences, might be particularized, which fall upon the tax-payer, in consequence of the modes in which a tax is levied, under this point of view, but the most considerable have been specified above and the reader will readily perceive any omissions when he recollects, that the object of all fiscal enactments ought to be, to transfer from each subject to the Government, a certain portion of his wealth, by the easiest and least complicated mode.

It is obvious that whenever the expenses of a State are paid by enforced contribution, the perfection of unvexatiousness, because all taxes must be imposed on property, persons, actions and commodities &c, and the means necessary to acquire a knowledge of their number, or value or both, will always be felt as an evil, which prevents in this instance, the loss of happiness from being reduced to nothing. However it must be remarked that traders and manufacturers hardly consider these inconveniences an evil, because they are enabled to charge for them in the price of the goods they sell and thus the imposts which involve them, when advanced by producers and distributors in the first instance, become according to our nomenclature interferent. The final purchasers do not feel them, and are often unaware of their existence. Such is the case with our indirect taxes in general. Their popularity arises from this, added to the circumstance, that the tax itself is hidden in the price paid for the goods, of which it forms a part.

In the case of a property tax, it is requisite to ascertain the quantum of wealth possessed by each individual by estimating the worth of the several items composing it. In the case of a tax on commodities, it is requisite, at one stage or other of their production or distribution to ascertain their number, and if the impost be ad valorem their value also. If at Hamburgh all the public expenses were formerly defrayed by a voluntary tax to which each person contributed what he thought fit, his own conscience determining the sum best proportioned to his means, the financial[1] system was perfectly invexatious.

As it can hardly be hoped that many other countries will find it in their

---

[1] [Norman inserted the word 'third' into Turner's fair copy at this point, but it seems to have been a slip and has been deleted here.]

power to dispense with forced imposts, we may be allowed to assume, that in addition to the loss of happiness arising from the sum transferred by the taxpayer to the Government, a certain degree of vexatiousness must usually be submitted to, our object therefore should be to reduce this inconvenience, to its smallest practical amount.

The price which the subject disburses for the protection of the laws, is composed of the totality of the several sums he pays, whether they be raised by one tax or a hundred. It signifies nothing to him as far as regards his fortune, supposing his industry remains unfettered, whether he pays so much to the customs, so much to the excise, so much to the assessed taxes, or whether an equal sum be exacted by one large tax. But it is very different with regard to the inconvenience and trouble which the payment of his contributions impose upon him; these multiply ceteris paribus in proportion to the absolute number and variety in kind, of the taxes which he is called upon to pay. Under this point of view then, it is desirable for him, that the number of imposts should be diminished as much as possible, and if any one could be found capable of yielding a sum, equal to the whole expenditure of Government, his interest would lead him to wish that this should be adopted to the exclusion of all others.

Chapter 14

Unevasibility

A tax is called unevasible, when it presents to the taxpayer the smallest means of escaping from the payment of it.

The perfection of this quality would be attained, if no taxpayer could avoid contributing to the wants of Government the full amount of the tax, supposing him not to be incapacitated by absolute inability.

No argument is required to enforce due attention to this quality, when weighing the comparative merits of different imposts, nor is it necessary to enter into detail in order that the reader may form a clear notion of it. A few observations as to the manner in which it may be best attained is all that can be wanted. The possession of this quality in any given tax will depend upon the ease of escape and the temptation to escape, but in comparing two or more taxes with reference to the latter point we must not forget to take into account the amount which these produce or are capable of producing.

Thus if those taxes will be least evasible, other things being equal, which call forth the least powerful motive to evasion on the part of those on whom they are levied, the indirect taxes on spirits malt and imported goods in England, where the amount after having been advanced by the capitalist is finally reimbursed in the price paid by the consumer, are preferable in this respect to the Droits réunis in France, where the producer pays the tax on articles destined for his own private use. The gain indeed to him who cheats the revenue is as great in one case as in the other, but then the trader who carries on business on a large scale can be exposed to a degree of watchful superintendence, which would be intolerable, if applied to private individuals; even if the expense was not an invincible objection to it. And besides the large merchant feels it to be his interest to preserve his character for fair dealing, both with the Government and the public; and is exposed moreover to the argus eyes of his rivals in business, who would never allow him to use unchecked, a ready means of underselling them.

Those taxes will be least evasible which are collected from the smallest number of persons, or corporations, or which are laid on commodities, usually landed and stored up in great receptacles. Thus in the case of the duty on tea, while the East India company was a trading body, no attempt, or even wish to defraud the exchequer was even suspected, and very little smuggling, comparatively speaking, can be carried on from the West India and London docks &c &c.

Among imposts on property and income those on land and houses, the public debt &c possess this quality in the highest perfection as they can neither escape observation nor be removed. Then come those on mortgages bond &c, which always may be and indeed ought even independently of all fiscal views, to be subjected to a general system of registration. Those on the capital or profits of traders are most liable to be evaded, as a reference to the returns from the income tax would evince, if experience were necessary to confirm so obvious a truth.

Other things being equal, the unpopularity and vexatiousness of a tax, increases its evasibility. The possession of these qualities are distinct evils imposed upon the taxpayer in addition to the money amount required from him and in proportion to the temptation to commit an act, will be the chance of its being committed.

It is necessary here to repeat an observation which was developed at some length in the chapter on computability and which ought to be kept in mind during any discussion upon the merits of rival imposts, vizt. Thus on comparing one or more together we must not satisfy ourselves with ascertaining the inconveniences attaching to each absolutely and then ranging them in the order which they appear to occupy under the first point of view; but must also take into account their productiveness, the sums they severally yield, are required to yield, or are capable of yielding, recollecting that evils which would be intolerable, if bringing to the exchequer only a small sum, might be hardly worth notice, if they were the means of producing a revenue a hundred or a thousand times as much. In other words, when examining into the qualities of one or more taxes their productiveness must always be kept in view. This characteristic is indeed so important, that it might have been selected as a separate quality, had it not been deemed expedient to make some sacrifice to brevity.

Part III

Review of Existing or Supposed Taxes

Chapter 15

Motives Influencing the Framers of Taxes

The last section contained a detailed account of the qualities which ought to exist in a good tax, the present will contain an examination of each of the principal branches of taxation. It will be our chief object to observe in what degree they fulfil the required conditions, or in other words, what is their effect upon public virtue and happiness. We have seen that taxation properly so called, is always an evil, because even when reduced to its lowest term, it must diminish the general felicity, by the amount of the power of purchasing enjoyment which it takes away from individuals; but we have seen also, that this sacrifice is richly recompensed by the protection of a regular Government, to the existence of which it is absolutely essential; and that all that is necessary to enable us to enjoy this protection with the slightest mixture of alloy, is to take care that the system of finance as a whole, and consequently the particular items that comprise it be rendered as far as possible, computable, simple, frugal, constant, divisible, popular noninterferent, equal, uncorruptive, unvexatious, and unevasible.

From what has been before said, it will appear that the adoption of two very simple rules will be sufficient to guide in a considerable degree the measures of the financier so as to prevent him, in most instances from diminishing unnecessarily the common happiness.

1. Reduce the expenditure to the lowest point which will support a Government calculated to afford protection to the subject.

2. Never to impose a tax for any other purpose than that of increasing the revenue by its whole amount.

It is only with the last of these rules, that this work has any necessary connexion; the ensuing examination of existing taxes will shew us that Governments in imposing them have frequently acted in defiance of it.

1. They have sometimes thought that they knew the economical interest of the Nation, better than the individuals which compose it, and have therefore given an unnatural direction to the national industry. When acting under this impression their motive has been to increase the National wealth.

2. Sometimes they have endeavoured by fiscal regulations to augment the defensive or aggressive means of the State. With this view they have imposed heavy duties on the exportation of munitions of war, or the raw material of which they are manufactured, or have enacted navigation laws. In this instance their motive has been to increase the political power of the Nation.

3. Sometimes they have interfered to diminish by extra taxation the consumption of commodities which they have thought likely to increase immorality. Here their motive has been a wish to diminish vice.

4. They have sometimes tried so to arrange their fiscal system as either to increase or diminish the use of some particular commodity or commodities so as to benefit peculiar individuals or classes. In this instance their object has been to enrich the favored persons.

These motives do not show themselves solely in the enactment of laws, which create what are called taxes; they very frequently appear in the shape of bounties, monopolies and prohibitions.

It is plain that the principles involved in them all contradict the two fundamental maxims already laid down; with the first maxim we have little to do, but before we proceed with the intended review, it may be advisable to consider, whether a Government ought even to modify its observance of the second, under any circumstances, and if at all, to what point a neglect of it can be expedient. This discussion need not be long; part of it has been already anticipated, and part of it will naturally find a place, when the nature and effects of particular taxes are examined.

The validity of the first motive can only be maintained upon a supposition which has been already shewn to be groundless. It is therefore merely necessary to observe in this place that whenever a legislature endeavours to increase the National wealth, by any other means than that of leaving capital and industry perfectly unfettered it invariably produces a directly contrary effect, and retards the march of public prosperity.

The framers of enactments upon this plan, cannot escape from the following dilemma, their regulations must either interfere with that direction which individual interest would give to industry, or they must not; in the first case they are hurtful, in the latter useless.

When the motive for a fiscal law is to raise the price of some particular commodity, and thus benefit the producers of that commodity at the expense of the rest of the community; the very existence of such an intention, or at least the power of acting upon it, shows that the Government does not proceed upon the principle that ought to regulate its conduct, instead of endeavouring to promote the greatest happiness of the greatest number, the course here adopted is to rob the many for the benefit of the few.

We have already seen that even the few will be injured, unless they are enabled to monopolize the production of the article, whose price has been

artificially raised, and prevent the competition of other capitalists, and that
without this they cannot ultimately obtain a higher profit than the common
rate, though the exchangeable value of the commodity they sell may have
doubled.

In every conceivable instance of a departure from the rule of leaving commerce unfettered, a diminution of national wealth is the result, or at least the
productive powers of capital and labor are weakened; we must now examine
whether or no this disadvantage can ever be counterbalanced by an increase
of the relative political power of the State.

In the solution of this as of all other problems connected with legislation, an appeal is to be made to the doctrine of utility. We must first enquire
whether the proposed measure will really increase the relative political power
of the State, and if at all, to what degree. Supposing the answer to be affirmative which can rarely, if ever be the case, we must examine whether the
diminution of public happiness, occasioned by the interference with the free
development of industry, be or be not more considerable than the increase of
it which will follow an augmentation of political power, which augmentation
must take place in the shape of greater security, for no wise Government,
could ever wish to encourage, in the minds of its subjects an appetite for
foreign domination, or that illiberal contempt and hatred for other Nations,
which usually accompany it. Thus then the question is reduced within a nar-
row compass, is the gain of security, preferable to the loss of wealth, and the
other inconveniences flowing from fiscal enactments? This question cannot
be answered, without an examination of examples, which would detain us too
long, and is the less necessary, as few can now be drawn from the practice
of this country. The navigation laws indeed exhibit the motive in question,
but then it is not carried into action through the medium of taxation. The
high duties on European timber constitute however a case in point.[1]   On

---

[1] [See note p. 189 on the timber duties.]

the whole it may be affirmed that a set of circumstances have hardly ever occurred, under this head, where a legislature ought to have lost sight of the rule, of never imposing a tax, for any other purpose than that of increasing revenue. Should such a case occur it will of course authorize a departure from it in the particular instance but in no other.

We must next examine the expediency of endeavouring to diminish immorality through the medium of taxation.

There can be no doubt that every legislature ought to foster virtue and diminish vice and crimes wherever it may be possible, for the end of legislation is to promote the common happiness, and every act of immorality necessarily involves a diminution of it.

The imposition of heavy duties on the production or importation of certain articles, which are supposed to act as the incentive to crimes, so as to raise their price and to place them beyond the reach of the greater number of individuals has been the usual mode, in which the motive now commented on has shewn itself.

Two questions therefore here present themselves to the reader's attention:

1. Is it possible to diminish the loss of happiness arising from immorality by fiscal regulations?.

2. Supposing the first question to be answered in the affirmative, is the gain of happiness, arising from a diminution of immorality in consequence of the tax, greater than the loss of happiness occasioned by the tax?

The most convenient method of solving the questions proposed, will be to select some example of such a tax as that above described, and to point out the consequences that flow from it.

Let us choose a heavy impost upon spirits, the good attending which, will of course consist in the lessening intoxication, and the crimes and misery that flow from it. The money received by the exchequer is not to be considered as part of this good, because should this measure be found inexpedient, it can never be difficult to devise other means of appropriating part of the wealth already existing to the purposes of the State.

The principal evils on the other hand are:

1. Interference – The unnatural application of capital and industry.

2. Corruptiveness – The incentives to smuggling, which of course act upon every individual, but particularly upon the poor and occasion a widely spread demoralization, from the intensity of the temptation, to a breach of the laws. In proportion to this temptation arises the necessity of strong preventive measures, which put the country to a heavy expense, to pay custom house and excise officers, lawyers to prosecute criminals, and soldiers to guard them; nor must we forget the sufferings of these unhappy beings, and their families, who are severely punished for acts to the commission of which the popular sanction, opposes little if any barrier.

Altogether it seems clear, that the taxes intended to diminish inebriety, even if partially successful, have hitherto created a greater mass of evil, than they have removed, and it may even be doubted whether they have produced any good affect whatever. In the United States spirits sell at perhaps a tenth of the price they bear in Great Britain, while the wages of labour are much higher, and yet it does not appear that drunkenness is more frequent in the former than in the latter country. In the greater part of Continental Europe also, fermented liquors are much cheaper in proportion to the means of purchase possessed by the mass, than here yet the working classes are more sober.

Even in this country intoxication is much less common among the rich, who have unbounded means of gratifying a taste for it than among the poor, who are supposed to be protected from the effects of their own passions by legislative interference. While the latter have become more temperate in the last few years, since the price of fermented liquors has fallen.

We must never also forget, that spirits may be applied to a good as well as a bad purpose, and that by raising their price immoderately, we equally prevent the one, as well as the other application of them.

Altogether it seems difficult to deny, that should the Government wish to diminish a practice either immoral in itself, or leading to the commission of immoral acts; it would act far more wisely as well as more efficaciously, by striving first to enlighten the people as to their real interest, and then by affixing specific penalties to the perpetration of such acts than by this species of indirect legislation. Whether it be expedient at all to punish intoxication criminally is another question, but there seems little doubt, that less evil would result from an attempt so to suppress it, than from raising immoderately the price of fermented liquors, through the medium of an excessive impost, and thus diverting a quantity of industry into a comparatively unproductive channel, and creating an enormous temptation to smuggling.

The reasoning employed to shew the impolicy of a very heavy tax on spirits, will apply to all other imposts of the same class, and on the whole we may safely conclude, that a desire to diminish immorality should seldom or ever occasion any modification of our rule; that the legislature imposing a tax should have no other view than to increase the revenue.

There is another class of taxes, that on luxuries, which though their motive be only to increase the revenue, are sometimes supposed to produce a beneficial effect, by lessening the consumption of articles not essentially necessary to the preservation of life.

This class has a certain connection with that which we have last considered and is exempt from many of the inconveniences which belong to them; little objection indeed can be made to the latter, when they form part of an heterogeneous mass of contributions, but it must not be forgotten that the word or idea of luxury, is one of the most vague, that can be imagined. It seems usually considered as denoting every thing beyond the necessaries, and simple conveniences which fall to the lot of laborers and artisans. In this sense its signification will vary from one year to another in the same country, and from one country to another at the same time.

On the whole it seems clear that we have done right in not enumerating among the good qualities of a tax, the power of contributing indirectly to the national wealth, defence or virtue, and that the legislator can hardly ever, if at all gain his end, when he attempts to forward these objects, through the medium of fiscal regulations.

Chapter 16

General Observations on Indirect Taxes

The effects of taxes may be considered under several points of view:

1. Those which are occasioned by the art of levying them.

2. Those which flow from their amounts and the application of their produce &c &c. The first only falls within the scope of this work, its chief object being to shew how any given sum may be raised with the smallest diminution of public happiness.

In order to simplify the intended review it will be convenient to adopt the common division of taxes into direct and indirect; though the terms are far from unexceptional, as some taxes belong to both classes. In the first division are included all those imposts, which are paid immediately, by the persons whom the legislator intends should finally pay them. Under the second, are included all the taxes, for which the immediate contributor is supposed to be reimbursed sooner or later. These are usually paid at one stage or other by the production or transport of commodities, and before they reach the consumer.

Indirect taxes may be divided into three classes:

1. Customs – Taxes collected at the frontiers on commodities imported from or exported to, foreign countries.

2. Excise – Taxes on commodities, collected in the interior, such commodities being usually produced or manufactured at home.

3. Indirect – Taxes falling under neither of the above heads, such as mercantile stamps, licences for the exercise of particular trades, the house and window tax under certain circumstances.

And these imposts thus classified may be each divided into:

1. Those falling upon articles more or less the objects of a monopoly.

2. Those falling on articles not produced under a monopoly. Each of these divisions require a few observations.

Articles produced under a monopoly more or less perfect form a more extensive class, than has commonly been imagined. They comprehend in addition to those which are accidental such as certain rare wines and those that have owed their origin to the erroneous policy of government all raw produce in old and long settled countries, where inferior qualities of land are cultivated.

Taxes imposed on such articles fall partly on the consumer, and partly on the monopolist in the first instance, and eventually perhaps wholly on the latter. This point will be carefully investigated hereafter, especially in the chapter on Tithes.

Taxes on articles into which monopoly does not enter *fall wholly on consumers, raising prices by their whole amount*, though these if labourers are usually reimbursed after a longer or shorter interval by a rise in wages.

Imposts on objects of luxury unmonopolized, are paid wholly and finally by those who make use of them, when monopolized the burthen is divided or thrown wholly on the monopolist.

Those on necessaries, so far as they affect labourers, are thrown on capitalists, though the medium of a rise in wages.

Taxes on articles used by traders and manufacturers, are merely advanced by them, and are finally paid by the consumer of the goods produced.

Customs and excise may again be divided into:

1. Those falling on luxuries.

2. Those falling on necessaries and raw produce.

The motives for establishing the indirect taxes have been various. All those enumerated in the last chapter whether wise or erroneous have entered into the contemplation of those who imposed them; they have opened the most spacious field, for an exhibition of the erroneous theories of Statesmen, and through their means the most serious inroads have been made on the wealth, the virtue and the happiness of the world.

Much of the evil occasioned practically by the indirect taxes, is not inherent in them; it might be mitigated though not entirely removed; still the ensuing analysis will shew, that they are eminently liable to abuse, and that a very high degree of skill is required in order to counteract their constant tendency to produce unnecessary evil.

The customs shall first occupy our attention. A general view of them will be exhibited in this chapter and they will be subjected to a more particular examination in the next.

In most countries they have been established with a view first of all to raise a revenue, then to insure an influx of the precious metals, and to protect what is called home industry, against the competition of foreigners, the two last of these objects being wholly opposed to all sound views of economical science. No writer of eminence now defends them, yet few are aware, of the extensive evils which they have occasioned. It were greatly to be wished that those who have it in their power to procure the requisite data would take the trouble of calculating according to the formula given in chapter 6, the absolute loss occasioned to such a country as Great Britain by this branch of her fiscal regulations, and contrast it with the amount paid into the exchequer. The eyes of the public would thus be opened, and those ameliorations which the Government wishes to introduce, but which it is unable to force against established interests might be called for by the popular voice.[1]

The fundamental mischief in the customs is, that they disturb the natural distribution of capital and labour. Besides the interference incident to them as now established, which arises from the intention of their framers to favor the consumption of one description of goods rather than another, there is an additional portion which has arisen partly from the ignorance of legislators, and partly from the very nature of the system on which these have acted. By affixing a certain impost, on all goods of a particular size or particular weight they have obliged the producers in foreign countries to prepare their merchandise as little below the prescribed size and weight as possible, perhaps at a great sacrifice in point of cost. These persons instead of studying only to please the consumer have been compelled in the first place to evade the tax, as far as they were able. Let us take an instance. The duty on planks is the same, whether they be 7 feet or 16 feet long, $1\frac{1}{2}$ inch or $3\frac{1}{2}$ inches thick, 8 inches or 14 inches wide, but of a great many trees cut down, not half in some countries may produce timber 16 feet long and of a good quality; or if a tree reach that length, it may and probably will, fall short of its next multiplicants 32 feet and 48 feet. Under the present system however, all planks much under 16 feet become unfit for the English market; yet the foreigner must nevertheless be paid for them, and he can only receive payment, by charging as much for the half he does send to England, as he would charge for the

---

[1] See Edinbr Review I think 1827 for loss in consequences of Protection – [The reference is to J.R. McCulloch 'Abolition of the Corn Laws', *Edinburgh Review* vol. 44, September 1826, pp. 319-59 at p. 341.]

whole, was he allowed to send the whole.[2]

This palpable example has been selected, because it aptly represents a numerous family of the same kind, and we may generalize the inference to be drawn from it, by recollecting that any useless expenditure, which our fiscal regulations impose on producers, must be finally reimbursed to them by the consumers in the additional price these are compelled to pay for the goods they purchase.

An ad valorem duty would remedy the above evil but would hardly even alleviate another of great magnitude, which is inherent in the very nature of a custom-house, the many delays, expenses and other vexations, to which merchants are exposed, in entering paying duty on, and discharging their cargoes. Every separate article must be weighed, measured or valued, they must only work a certain number of hours in each day, and their ships must be unloaded in particular harbours or even in particular docks. All this must be endured and paid for, in addition to the real prime cost and duty, in order to prevent the revenue from being defrauded.

Foreign goods are sold in general at a price just sufficient to reimburse the exporters and to afford them the common rate of profit, in the country where they are produced. It follows that any imposition of duty either in the producing or importing country, must raise the price by an amount at least equal to the tax, unless where the article is the produce of a monopoly. But it may perhaps happen that the inhabitants of the importing country may be either unable or unwilling to consume as large a quantity of goods at the advanced price as they did before hence follows a diminution of consumption, and a probable disappointment in the extent of the expected revenue. It is thus impossible to calculate before hand, what will be gained to the exchequer

---

[2][On the timber trade see note p. 189. Norman joined the family timber business on leaving Eton in 1810, and remained in it, becoming its guiding force. He made a number of trips to Norway in connection with the business, and in particular with attempts to recover debts owed to the firm. He retired from the firm shortly after the death of his father, which occurred in January 1830, and his own marriage in October of that year.]

by the increase of an existing, or the establishment of a new duty.

Supposing a certain quantity of any article to pay £55 – and that this impost be doubled, it will generally be found that the produce subsequently will be less than double. On the other hand, should it be diminished to £25, the produce will be more than half what it was before. This is the ordinary, but not the inevitable state of things. It may happen that a further advance of duty will augment the revenue in a similar ratio. But as such a measure can have no tendency to augment national wealth it must necessarily in a country where most commodities are taxed, diminish the consumption of some other taxed commodity, and consequently the gain to the exchequer derived from it.

But supposing that the legislature neither increases or diminishes duties, it by no means follows, that they shall produce neither more or less than the expected amount. The taste or the wants of consumers may alter, or prices may rise in consequence of a rise in the costs of production, and consumption be checked, or the costs of production may be lowered, and a contrary effect take place.

It may indeed be said that in a country like Great Britain, the whole produce of the Customs may be predicted at any time with tolerable accuracy for the ensuing year – be it so. Yet we must recollect that all the terms by which we designate the qualities of things are relative and that this prediction may and usually will fail in its accomplishment, either on the side of excess or deficiency. If then any other large system of taxes can be considered and which possess in a much higher degree than Customs and Excise duties the quality of consistency and computability, which cannot in practise produce more or less than the legislator intends, or fall on other persons than those he wishes to pay them, we should be justified in choosing them in preference to the latter. It must also be considered that the possession of the above qualities in a tolerable degree can be only predicated on the whole mass of Custom House duties – the duty on one particular article in practice varying though a sort of rough compensation may go far to equalise the final results.

In addition to the inconveniences already mentioned custom house duties when their rates are increased or diminished, produce the bad effect of occasioning an export or import of the precious metals; thus altering the value of the currency, and unsettling contracts, and all the relations of debtor and creditor. A country producing a commodity in which a new export duty has been imposed, cannot export it in such quantity as before, or ceases to export it altogether. Merchants are therefore obliged to pay in money for articles previously obtained in barter for such goods. The quantity of money is therefore lowered in the country where the article is produced, the value of it is raised, and along with this effect appears an increased power of purchasing on the part of the Government, and of individuals possessed of fixed money incomes, all those who owe money lose, all those who are owed money gain. This state of things continues until all the precious metals, which the one country can furnish, are extracted from it, or until the fall of prices there added to the rise in the country formerly importing the taxed commodity restore the equilibrium between their respective currencies.

A duty on importation produces a directly contrary effect on the distribution of the precious metals. It occasions an accumulation of them in the country imposing it. The nation which before exported the taxed commodity, is obliged for a time to send gold and silver to a greater or less extent instead of it. Money prices rise[3] where the duty is levied. Debtors gain and creditors lose, in the above instances, the customs are unequal.

Some persons may consider it extraordinary that in the arguments hitherto employed it has been assumed that duties on imported articles are usually paid by the country imposing them, this is sufficiently true for the purposes of general reasoning; as it is only incorrect, where the articles in question are produced under a system of monopoly, or where for a short time,

---

[3] [Norman's manuscript has 'fall'.]

foreign producers are able or willing to sell at a loss, instead of transferring the whole or part of their capitals to some more profitable employment. Such a state of things can be but transient. The monopoly however may be permanent.

We are often told indeed, in answer to any observations upon the worthlessness of our transmarine possessions that the Island of Jamaica for instance yields us an annual revenue of two to three million, and upon a doubt being expressed, as to the correctness of this opinion, we are referred to the amount of duty collected from the sugar coffee &c imported from that colony. Now how does the matter really stand? Jamaica sends us her produce, which costs us more than the same quantity of tropical commodities would cost, if our merchants were allowed to buy them in the cheapest markets. Upon the produce so imported a duty is paid which is reimbursed to the merchant by the consumer in England and increases the price he has to pay by its full amount. Was not the latter called upon to contribute in this way to the revenue, the sum raised by the sugar duty would remain in his pocket, whence it might be readily extracted for the public service by some other species of impost. It is true indeed that were the sugar duty under present circumstances lowered the revenue of the planter would be raised, he would pocket a portion of the duty remitted. This is owing to the monopoly of the market, which is afforded him by our existing legislation. We first raise his income by excluding foreign sugars, and then take a portion of this income in the shape of an extravagant import duty. It would be wiser to lower the duty, and to admit the produce of other tropical countries on equal terms.

It is not a little remarkable, and can be attributed only to the importance, which was formerly attached to the creation of what was called a favorable balance of trade, that the means by which foreigners can be most easily made to pay any thing towards the revenue have been almost wholly neglected. These means consist of duties on exportation. Should a country possess any peculiar advantages in the production of a particular commodity, so as to be able to sell it much cheaper than any other country, she might impose a duty upon it, which would be wholly paid by foreigners. This duty might be fixed at such a rate, as would increase the price, until only a sufficient inducement was left for its exportation. Suppose that a particular sort of cotton goods of great general utility could be manufactured in England at 2s per yard, and not at less than 5s in Germany, the expense of transport being 6d per yard. In this case an export duty of 2s per yard might be laid upon the goods in question which would be wholly paid by the Germans. They would buy the cottons although at a cost of 4s/6d per yard, as they could not by the supposition manufacture for themselves under 5s. Did no duty exist, they would obtain them from England at the price current here with the addition of the cost of transport, that is for 2s/6d per yard.

The duty on coals exported to foreign countries was a tax which fell wholly on the purchasers and its late abolition must be considered uncalled for and impolitic.

It would seem then that custom house duties, did they exist at all, should affect exported as well as imported goods. The advantage last described however, though it belongs to them almost exclusively in the wide circle of taxation, can operate extensively in so few instances, and may be so easily destroyed by countervailing duties in foreign countries on the goods which these export, that it affords no sufficient recompense for the evils of this species of taxation.

Chapter 17

Custom House Duties

It will now be proper to consider the effect of Custom House Duties when divided according to the second plan of classification alluded to in chapter 16:

1. Those on the commodities consumed chiefly by laborers, or which constitute the raw materials of manufacturers,

2. On articles chiefly consumed by the richer classes.

We have already remarked that taxes falling upon commodities not produced under a monopoly, raise their price nearly by the amount of the tax. When these are consumed by landlords or annuitants therefore they are paid out of rent or fixed incomes, when by laborers they first abridge the slender portion of comforts previously enjoyed by the laboring class, and should no permanent degradation in the condition of the latter ensue fall eventually on profits. When by capitalists the sacrifice is imposed immediately on them.

Duties on articles employed in manufactures which form no considerable part of the laborer's expenditure, and duties on luxuries, do not raise wages or sink profits, and consequently fall wholly, on consumers or monopolists.

Sir Henry Parnell in his excellent work on financial reform expatiates with great earnestness on the bad effects produced by taxes on the raw materials of manufacturers. Many of his observations on this head are founded on correct principles, but he does not seem sufficiently to feel that their abolition and the substitution of imposts on rent and fixed incomes would expose our fiscal system to a charge of the most revolting inequality. It may be wise in the infancy of a financial establishment to adopt as a maxim the abandonment of all taxes on production, but it can hardly be just to act on such a maxim for the first time at its maturity when all the arrangements of Society have been made on an opposite plan.

Many persons are in error in supposing that loss to the public arises from the payment of the tax, in an early stage of the process of production, because when finally paid by the consumer it is loaded with the profit charged by the producer on his advances. They do not recollect, that in this case, the delay is a gain to the latter, for which the augmented price is no more than a fair equivalent.

Taxes on raw materials are, indeed eminently objectionable, when they are interferent and vexatious, when they impose shackles on the producer and thus cost him more than their money amount, of which there are too many instances as Sir Henry Parnell has shewn, but this fault is not inherent in all of them, and if indirect taxes are to exist at all, there seems no sufficient reason why all raw materials should be exempted from them. It cannot be shewn that in all cases these cost the community more than they bring to the revenue added to the same amount of expense in collection, as belongs to other indirect imposts.

The entire mass of imposts reviewed in this chapter are grossly unequal, except when levied at one rate ad valorem. Those on necessaries and raw produce in their first operation abridge the comforts of the laborer, who ought never to be called upon for a pecuniary sacrifice to State purposes. After an equalisation has taken place, and wages have risen so as exactly to meet the increased price in the articles on which these are expended, these taxes fall almost wholly on profits, and do not therefore deduct a nearly equal proportionate share from the enjoyments of every class and individual possessing wealth in the community. In order to attempt to balance this evil we may impose a direct tax on rent and fixed incomes; this will be to balance one unequal tax, by another unequal tax. Who can tell exactly, the reduction on rent or which shall exactly compensate, for the loss to the capitalist arising from higher wages, consequent upon an increase, in the price of raw produce and necessaries.

Both the customs and excise in England are usually levied at a far higher rate on the cheaper description of commodities consumed by the poor than on the more costly articles that fall to the share of the rich. Thus gin pays, at the prime cost about 900 per cent, champagne 108 per cent. Ordinary tobacco 1200 per cent. cigars 105 per cent. This is a revolting instance of inequality, and should be corrected without delay, though a rise of wages may have somewhat compensated for its effects.[1]

Taxes on imported luxuries are also very unequal. No person need pay them, unless he thinks proper, he may give up that pleasure which their use was calculated to afford him. But why should the Government call upon any particular set of individuals to make these peculiar sacrifices? Let us take the instance of a tax on wine. A drinks only water, and has no wish for any other beverage. B likes wine, and finds it beneficial to his health. A tax on wine then falls wholly on B though he may be by far the poorer man of the two. After the imposition of the tax his happiness is diminished, whether he continues to purchase wine or abstains from the use of it, while the enjoyments of A are untouched.

---

[1] See Westminster Review for 1834. [The figures in this paragraph were omitted in Norman's Ms. They have been supplied here from the article to which Norman referred, 'Aristocratic Taxation', *Westminster Review* Vol. 21, no. 41, July 1834, art ix pp. 140-85. The article contains no reference to the duty on champagne, but gives a figure of 108 per cent for the duty on wine, in making the same point as Norman. On the basis of internal evidence, the article has been attributed to John Crawford. See W.E. and E.R. Houghton *The Wellesley Index to Victorian Periodicals* Vol. 3 Toronto: University of Toronto Press, 1979, p. 580.]

Even granting the propriety of taxing luxuries who shall specify exactly
the commodities, which ought to be included under that name. And when
we have succeeded in making a catalogue of them, how few in number shall
we find them? And how inconsiderable will be the revenue, which it will
be possible to raise upon them? For it must be recollected that if the tax
upon them exceeds a certain amount, consumption of the taxed articles will
wholly cease, and the happiness of the community be diminished without
any addition to the revenue.

Custom house duties are not that class of imposts, of which the diminution or abolition is demanded with most earnestness by public opinion, and a
similar remark maybe made with respect to indirect taxes in general. Taken
altogether they must be considered popular. Yet this favorable circumstance
is founded in a great degree on misapprehension. The immediate payers
know and feel that they are reimbursed for all their advances in the augmented price which they are enabled to charge for their goods, and that, was
the duty abolished, they would be compelled immediately by the effects of
competition to sell for so much less, in other words that the tax costs them
nothing, and perhaps in some instances, owing to the mode in which it is
levied, creates a petty monopoly in their favor while the more numerous class
of consumers loses sight of the impost in the general cost of the articles purchased which may be abstained from altogether, should the taste or means of
any particular individual demand such a sacrifice. Thus the disbursements
for state purposes, assume the appearance of a voluntary contribution, and
the general result is that one million raised by property or assessed taxes,
will occasion more dissatisfaction than five times that sum levied by duties
on tea and sugar, which really diminish the means of enjoyment, so far as
money is concerned, in more than an equal proportion. The general spread
of enlarged views, will more and more correct these erroneous judgments,
but while they exist, the legislator will be compelled, and indeed ought in
some respects to humor them.

Under another point of view however public opinion regards the custom house duties &c with a less favorable eye, and they appear decidedly unpopular. The extreme ease with which they are evaded, the temptation they hold out to every member of the community, and the severity of the punishment reserved for those who infringe them, enlists the popular feeling, not in favor of the law, but in favor of those who break it. The greater part of the community regard the smuggler with approbation and rejoice in his success; while even those, who have reflected more seriously, on the advantages of Government, and the duty of providing for its expenses; or whose morality is of a less pliable cast, behold his offence without indignation, and look at his sufferings with pity. The man who should be detected in making false returns of his income, would be pronounced only one degree less criminal, than he who had defrauded his neighbour in one of the ordinary transactions of life, but the smuggler may glory in the success of his enterprises, the sympathy of his hearers would be usually excited in his favor, and his private character will suffer in the opinion of but few. It is unnecessary to expatiate on the grounds of these anomalies, they do not lie deep.

A tax should afford the slightest possible means or motives for evasion. Other things being equal, this minimum of evil is attained when it falls upon, and can be eluded by the smallest possible number of persons, without becoming unequal. All taxes must finally be paid by landowners, capitalists, and the owners of fixed incomes out of rent and profits, with the exception of that comparatively small portion which now fall on laborers unjustly as has been already shewn. It follows that the public contributions should fall on the three first classes in such a way, as to give no interest or power to any other persons to evade them. This reasoning, seems clear and undeniable. Now the customs like all other taxes ought to be, and usually are paid, by landowners, capitalists and annuitants, who hardly form a larger proportion of the whole community than from $\frac{1}{3}$rd to $\frac{1}{10}$th: while the temptation to evade them, extends not only to these persons but to the laborers, in fact to the whole aggregate of individuals, who form the nation.

Having thus given a general view of the customs, and pointed out the mode in which they injure public happiness beyond the mere money amount which they abstract from the people, this chapter will conclude with a short summary, in which their several evils will be pointed out in the order which has been adopted, in describing the characteristic qualities and which has been neglected in the preceding remarks, in order to make them more free from technicalities.

The customs are incomputable because the legislator who enacts them, cannot tell, either the amount they will produce, on whom they will fall, or when they will be paid, he can predict in fact only a portion of their effects, and those imperfectly. The payers share in his ignorance.

They are complex, because in comparison with the sum they yield, or are capable of yielding, they demand on the part of the payer and collector, a great number of separate acts, some of which are difficult and laborious.

They are prodigal in collection, this follows of necessity from their complexity &c. Their net produce 1831 was £15,336,000. Expenses £1,053,000, or about $6 - 6\frac{3}{4}$ per cent.[2]

They are inconstant from the change in seasons, in political circumstances, and in the taste and means of consumers.

They are indivisible, because no rule can be laid down which will measure before hand their increase or diminution, so as to make them furnish exactly what the legislator requires.

---

[2] [Norman's figure for Customs revenue was taken from pp. 12-13 of Marshall's tables, lines 71-2. It was the figure for 'Payments into the Exchequer' of £15,336,716 for 1831, rather than the gross revenue of £16,688,586 (line 38). The expenses figure is taken from ibid. p. 22 line 64, 'Management', where the figure is £1,053,834. This does indeed yield a collection cost of 6.4 per cent of the total of expenses plus payments into the Exchequer. However, Norman omitted a number of lesser expenses. For 1831 these were £26,092 (quarantine), £87,073 (warehousing), and £3,017 (coastal blockade). When these are taken into account the collection cost as a percentage of net revenue plus costs rises to 7.1 per cent.]

They must on the whole be considered as very popular. In the United States where the public voice has the greatest effect, they have been retained when all direct and internal imposts have been, abolished.

They are interferent when levied by weight or tale [number] to a very high degree, so that under this head, they have perhaps inflicted more evil on mankind than any other taxes. Equal duties ad valorem are most free from this fault.

They are unequal in a very high degree as they do not even make an attempt to tax the subject in proportion to his wealth.

They are peculiarly corruptive; official oaths, smuggling, disregard of the law &c &c.

They are not vexatious to the final payer, as he disburses their amount, frequently without being aware of it, they are however eminently vexatious to the immediate payer who is reimbursed for this loss as for others, in the price of the commodity, thus the final payer loses money instead of time and trouble and the tax becomes interferent according to our nomenclature.

They are evasible in a high degree; being collected from an almost infinite number of separate articles, many of which may readily be withdrawn from observation, while though collected from only a small number of persons, every person in the community, and even foreigners, may gain by eluding them.

Chapter 18

The Excise Monopolies

The full examination bestowed on the indirect taxes generally, and the customs in particular in the previous chapters of this section, will render it unnecessary to employ much time, on the next great branch of indirect taxes, the excise, which has been defined to consist of duties levied in the interior on articles usually produced or manufactured at home. There were indeed, and perhaps still are some imposts comprehended under this name in England, as well as in other countries, which are collected in the interior on commodities brought from abroad, which have not undergone any change since their importation. Such imposts differ only in name from the customs, except in so far, as their effects are modified by the mode of collection, in other respects the reasoning employed in the preceding chapters will exactly apply to them.

And here it is advisable to remark on the absurdity of collecting one part of the tax on a commodity at the frontier and another in the interior. The immediate consequence of course is to augment the expense of collection, the change of evasion &c &c.

The plan of laying successive duties on the same commodities at different steps during the process of manufacture, as was or is done in England with respect to malt, hops, beer, and Spirits affords an analogous instance of contempt for science and reason.

The excise is partially replaced in some countries, by the profit made by the Government on the manufacture or sale of certain articles, as tobacco, salt, gunpowder, opium &c. These monopolies will therefore be reviewed in the present chapter.

The reader is referred to the preceding chapters for the different effects of taxes on necessaries and raw produce and luxuries.

The legitimate motive, vizt. a desire to increase the revenue, has usually prompted the establishment of the excise. Still occasionally a desire to diminish immorality, or to benefit particular individuals or classes, has also entered into the scope of the legislator. From the diminished prevalence of erroneous motives we might conclude a priori that the excise was less pernicious than the customs, and the ensuing examination will be found to confirm the anticipation.

The excise is also preferable to the customs from the circumstance that it falls in a greater number of instances upon articles produced under a monopoly. A list of imposts thus characterized which comprehends those on malt, hops &c will be found in the general table in the appendix.[1] They would be unequal if newly established, but cannot be considered unequal, when they have existed during a long period.

If the malt tax were to be abolished barley after a certain interval would probably rise to the present price of malt, minus the expense of manufacture, and its whole amount would then have been transferred to the landowner in the shape of rent. The abolition of the corn laws could alone justify such a measure by making it generally beneficial to the public.

One reason why the abolition of the leather tax has given so little relief to the consumer, is that skins are an object of the landed monopoly. In this instance however the effect could have been but small, as even the whole impost added but little to the price of a pair of shoes.

The excise is however no less incomputable than the customs. But a

[1][This appendix, and the table referred to by Norman here, have not been found amongst the Norman papers at Maidstone.]

small portion of its effects can be predicted, and those imperfectly. It also resembles the other great branch of the indirect taxes in complexity. The acts and regulations which its repartition and collection necessitated are numerous and difficult.

In this country at present the excise differs little from the customs in point of prodigality, it was formerly superior to them. In the year 1831 the gross sum it raised upon the people of Great Britain was £169,000,000 and the expense of collection £968,000 or about $5\frac{5}{7}$ per cent, the net receipt was about £14,300,000. We have seen that the expense of collecting the customs was about $6\frac{4}{5}$ths per cent.[2]

The excise duties are inconstant and indivisible. What has been said of the customs in chapter 17, will equally apply to them. They contain within themselves the same elements of popularity as the customs, though the degree in which they are subject to it, depends upon certain peculiar circumstances, in their administration which vary in different countries. In Spain and France, the internal taxes on consumption are more unpopular than those collected at the frontier, in Great Britain they are less so. If we examine these differences in the popular judgment, we shall find that the unpopularity of a tax other things being equal, increases in a direct ratio, with the extent and intensity of the temptation to evade it, the ease with which it may be eluded, and the number of persons called upon directly to pay it. In Great Britain the principal imposts of this description, those on

---

[2] [Norman's figure of £16,900,000 corresponds to the figure for total gross Excise receipts given by Marshall op. cit. pp. 14-15 line 28 where it is £16,900,264. However this is not the figure corresponding to the one for Customs which Norman employed above. It is 'Total Gross Receipts', rather than 'Payments into the Exchequer' (lines 51-2) which Norman quoted for the Customs. Payments into the Exchequer in respect of Excise duty in 1831 were reported by Marshall to be £14,380,875. Norman's calculation of expenses was taken from lines 42, 44, 45 and 46 of Marshall's table, presumably because there was no management figure as there was in the case of Customs. These expenses totalled £968,341, comprising £91,786 superannuation, £12,500 pensions, £5,734 bounties, and £858,321 salaries and allowances. These figures in total amount to 5.7 per cent of the gross figure of £16,900,264. But as a percentage of 'Payments into the Exchequer', which would provide a comparison with the Customs, it is 6.7 per cent.]

malt, spirits, glass &c, are collected in one stage or other of the process of production or just when it is completed, and before the commodity passes into the hands of the consumer. Now as these articles are manufactured by a comparatively small number of great capitalists, all that is necessary to prevent smuggling, is to place the establishments of the producers under the surveillance of the agents of Government. That being done it becomes almost impossible, that any considerable quantity of the article can find its way into the different channels of distribution, upon which the demands of the State have not been satisfied, while at the same time, no direct claim is made on the mass of the people.

On the other hand upon the continent, universally in former times, and to a great extent now, the excise was and is levied during the distribution. Barriers are erected at the gates of cities, or upon the roads leading from one province to another for the purpose of collection. We cannot fail here to recognize the superior wisdom of the British system.

In considering the degree in which the excise is unpopular, we must thus divide it, into duties on production as in England, on consumption and distribution as in France, and we must again distinguish the taxes on commodities which require in their manufacture, expensive and complex machinery and those which may be produced in any peasants hut.

The excise duties are interferent, the greater part of commodities are not exposed to them at all, while they fall upon others in very different proportions. In this respect however, they are greatly superior to the customs; the old doctrines as to the balance of trade, protection to home industry &c &c, leading to erroneous motives in the legislator could not usually be applied to them.

It is to be remarked, that if these several taxes were to be so altered as to bear about an equal proportion to the selling price of the articles on which they fell, the advantage obtained, though great would not be permanent, for the costs of production, and consequently the selling price of commodities are incessantly varying and any fixed amount of tax, would soon lose its intended proportion, and become either too high or too low.

The inconvenient and unscientific processes forced upon producers in order to render the collection more easy, as is the case with the excise on malt, spirits and glass in England, is another element of interference, and shews itself in the increased price and inferior quality of the article sold.

After all that is possible has been done to improve it many delays, vexations and expenses necessarily attend a tax on production, distribution, or consumption. Levy the tax ad valorem, or at a certain fixed amount for each article, and you still render it indispensable, that the whole process should be carried on under the eyes of the officers of Government. You still interfere with the convenience of individuals and introduce a crowd of evils, which would be excusable, only if they were inevitable, if they were a condition absolutely required, in order that a nation might enjoy the blessings of Government. Of the two kinds of excise duties particularized a few pages back, the first that upon necessaries falls upon consumers as far as it raises prices, upon capitalists, as far as it raises wages, and as landlords are only comprehended among the first named class, as they are indeed benefitted by whatever increases the price of raw produce, we may safely pronounce taxes upon necessaries, to be grossly unequal. When first imposed, and before wages have risen in exact proportion, we have repeatedly observed that they inflict a great deal of injustice, by obliging the laborer to endure a longer or shorter period of distress and privation.

The second kind of excise duties, fall wholly on consumers, except when imposed upon a monopolized article, and are also unequal because they do not even attempt to deduct an equal proportionate amount from the means of the taxpayers.

The excise like the customs is corruptive and evasible, but not in this country vexatious. owing.

1. To the small number of persons from whom it is collected.

2. To the circumstance that these persons endure the trouble and inconvenience it imposes in the regular course of their business and are paid for them.

The Droits réunis in France, and similar taxes in other parts of the continent, are levied directly on a large proportion of all householders and are perhaps more vexatious than any other imposts whatever. They become thus in great part direct taxes.

The reader is referred to chapter 16 and that on tithes for the principles involved in a tax on an article subject to a natural monopoly. Great care is required either in imposing or removing such a tax, as in the first case an unequal burthen may be thrown upon individuals; in the second they may derive the greater part of an advantage designed for the whole community. Thus supposing the malt tax of 20s a quarter to be abolished, it is probable that the price of barley would be permanently raised, by the extra demand 10s per quarter, and that thus one half of the tax would go into the pockets of the landowners, in the shape of increased rents, or be thrown away in the cultivation of inferior soils. This measure then would be highly inexpedient, even could the exchequer bear it, unless accompanied by a partial abolition of the corn laws.

Enough has been said upon the excise, as it exists in this country, we must now bestow some attention on certain indirect imposts, which resemble it in their nature, though bearing a different name.

In France, Spain, and Italy, the Government manufactures all the tobacco &c &c consumed, and fixes so high a price upon it, as to raise from the sale, a considerable revenue. The difference between the cost of the commodity to the State, and the price obtained for it, is of course a tax upon consumers. The supposed advantage obtained by this plan, is that smuggling becomes more difficult than if the fabrication was left in the hands of private persons.

This supposed advantage however vanishes before the test of experience, for notwithstanding the multiplication of severe punishments; the temptation is too strong to be resisted, the revenue is defrauded, and the prisons and galleys are crowded with malefactors.

Wherever the State carries on any branch of commerce, one result is certain and invariable, vizt. that the article produced, is dearer and worse, than if its preparation were left to the efforts of private ingenuity. The difference between what it does cost, and what it would cost, under a system of free trade, quality considered, is so much added to the tax, and may be considered an increase to the cost of collection. By this amount at least, such imposts on the continent are less frugal than the corresponding taxes here.

Had nature confined this species of manufacture to one particular district of each kingdom, and was the process of production simple, as is the case with salt in England, the objections against the plan in question would be less cogent, but even then probably our system would be preferable.

The Gabelle in France before the revolution, was a tax imposed through the medium of a sort of monopoly of salt; each household was supposed to require a certain quantity, and was compelled to pay for it, whether consumed or not. The mode of collecting the imposts and the regulations relating to it, were in the highest degree vexatious, burdensome and unequal. Through its means the prisons were filled, and the peasantry horribly oppressed, in short hardly any one circumstance tended more strongly to render the Government hateful and to hasten on the revolution than the misery arising from the operation of the Gabelle. It could hardly be looked upon as an indirect tax, inasmuch as the Government sold to the immediate consumer. Still as that was a circumstance of arrangement we may without impropriety notice it here along with others, to which it is in other respects so closely allied.

The revenue derived by the East India company from the sale of opium, resembles those lately criticized, except that the article produced is a slow poison; the use of it being generally followed by a premature death, preceded by an interval of acute suffering. The commodity is indeed exported for the most part to a foreign State, whose inhabitants therefore pay the tax. This distinction is doubtless a favorable circumstance in an economical point of view, but would not render the impost less corruptive in the eyes of the philanthropist or induce him to consider the legislator who retains it, as less stained with the guilt of a profound and selfish immorality, supposing that the trade is fostered by the Government, for the sake of the revenue it yields. It is said that the quantity of opium smuggled into Canton is sufficient to satisfy four millions of professed opium consumers, and that the number of these increases yearly. Who can hear this, without feelings of horror and disgust? But it may be asked, supposing the East India company to abandon the opium monopoly, would not that pernicious drug still continue to be sent to China, and would not its consumption be greatly increased, owing to the low price consequent upon free competition? Even supposing the cultivation of the poppy in the territories of the company to be prohibited effectually, would not an increase of cultivation in other parts of the world speedily supply the deficiency? A knowledge of facts is wanting to enable us to answer all these questions satisfactorily, but could an affirmative reply be given to them all, the judgment we should pass upon this part of the financial system of India would be considerably modified.

Chapter 19

Taxes on Particular Classes or Persons

Taxes on persons exercising certain particular employments, have sometimes arisen from the popular prejudices of a barbarous age, having been designed to throw a disproportionate share of the public burden upon a few obnoxious individuals. In some instances a wish to diminish immorality has also actuated their framers, while in others the object of the legislature has been simply to increase the revenue.

It often happens in England, that these taxes assume the shape of fees of office, in which case their produce does not usually go to the National exchequer, but becomes the perquisites of certain public servants.

This mode of applying the amount levied on contributions by no means alters the nature of the tax, except as it leads to extravagance and waste, to small service greatly overpaid, or to large emoluments, where no service whatever is yielded in return.

A tax levied on a particular trade or profession is transferred wholly to those who purchase the goods or services sold by the persons exercising such trade or profession, this is obvious because the general rate of profit having a tendency to equalize itself, he whose profits are reduced by what he is called upon to pay to the State below the common level, will raise his prices, or endeavour, should he fail in this, to divert his industry into some other channel. Even should he not succeed at once, the effect will only be delayed. A smaller number of beginners than before will enter upon the employment which is no insufficiently remunerated, and the equilibrium be restored by a diminished supply.

Even in this case the effect would be produced within a short time, after the tax had been imposed.

It must be observed however that the above reasoning applies to a partial, not a general tax. If a tax were to be levied on all traders and professional men or even on a large majority, the burden would fall on them, not on consumers.

These partial taxes are greatly deficient in computability, constancy and divisibility. As at present regulated, it is impossible to predict what they will produce, or on whom they will fall, or to vary their produce according to the varying wants of the State. They are however simple. The fact that an individual exercises a particular employment may be easily ascertained, and when that has been done nothing remains, but to demand a certain fixed sum from him; yet they are in general prodigal, in some instances unnecessarily so. The duty on hawkers and pedlars cost in collection in 1828 £13. 8.7 per cent, the produce being £77,400, the expenses £22,400.[1] This arose from the preposterous plan which had been adopted of creating a particular office for the management of so inconsiderable a branch of the revenue.

They are not unpopular. Before their transference to the purchasers of commodities or services, the original, who in that case are the ultimate payers, form too inconsiderable a body to interest the public sympathy against

---

[1] See Sir H. Parnell p.123. [Parnell, 1831 op. cit. chapter ix p. 119 'Stamp Duties'. The gross revenue figure was £77,437 and the cost of collection was given as £13. 18s. 7d. per cent. A cost of collection of 13.93 per cent would thus have amounted to nearly £10,787, reducing the net yield to £66,650. However, Parnell was reporting the results of taxing hackney carriages as well as pedlars, and although he does indeed put the percentage cost of collection at the figure quoted, he also reports that the net revenue was only £55,000. Given a gross revenue of £77,437, this implies a collection cost not of 13.93 per cent but of 28.97 per cent.]

their peculiar grievances. When transferred to consumers, as is the usual case, they share in that favor, which is shewn to most indirect taxes; buyers do not know or at least soon forget, the burden thus imposed upon them.

Disproportionate taxes on particular employments, act precisely like disproportionate taxes on particular commodities; they are interferent, they prevent the free distribution of capital and labor, and may sometimes occasion a sacrifice to the community which far outweighs the revenue they produce to the exchequer.

When first established they are usually unequal, as to the persons immediately called upon to pay them. These will probably be unable for some time to throw the burden off their own shoulders, their profits will sink below the common rate, some may even be obliged to abandon their employments with the loss of a considerable portion of their means, certainly with the sacrifice of that moral capital of skill and aptitude, which study and experience have given them. When an equalization takes place, the inequality falls upon the persons who purchase the commodities or services from those immediately paying the tax. They no longer contribute to the service of the State in proportion to their wealth, and in some instances the injustice they suffer is peculiarly glaring. Consider the situation of such as are obliged to have recourse to the temporary succour afforded by the pawnbroker, already weighed down by the pressure of calamity; their necessities oblige them knowingly to submit to a great sacrifice for immediate subsistence and support. Is it not the height of cruelty and oppression, to snatch from them even the smallest portion of that relief for which they must necessarily pay so high a price? Compare the loss they sustain with the gain to the exchequer, and then decide whether such a source of revenue should be suffered any longer to exist. Many instances of a similar kind might be found.

In this way they become to a certain degree corruptive, by increasing the cost of useful services of the best quality, they hold out an inducement to individuals, not to purchase such services. In some cases they oblige the poor man, to have recourse to the pettifogger or the quack instead of the respectable legal or medical practitioner, or may compel him altogether to abandon a just demand, or to neglect his health.

The fees on the enrollment of attorneys are in fact law taxes, and as such though mentioned now will be particularly examined hereafter. See chapter 10.

These taxes cannot be considered either vexatious or evasible.

In conclusion it may be remarked, that the fees levied by certain corporations are often used as the means of creating a sort of monopoly against the public, and thus impose a tax much heavier than their apparent amount, in the shape of extravagant emoluments to the favored, and probably unworthy few, besides the additional loss, arising from the effect of a diminished competition on the amount and average of skill and talent employed.

The Droit des Patentes in France is much heavier, and extends to more trades, and professions, than any imposts of the same kind in England, to so many indeed that it probably falls on the immediate payers, and not on the consumers. It would occupy too much time to attempt a particular description of it, and the materials for one are not easily attainable.

Chapter 20

Direct Taxes on Objects of Luxury

The regular distribution of the subject, now brings us to the family of direct taxes, or such as are paid in the first instance by those whom the legislature intends shall finally contribute to them. Some of these taxes are in fact indirect, and might have been enumerated in the last chapters; but less inconvenience will arise from maintaining the ordinary arrangement, than from the adoption of a new one, more strictly scientific.

Having determined to retain the common classification as to the direct and indirect taxes, we now proceed to pass the former in review, and for the sake of clearness and precision shall place them under different heads. The subject of this chapter will be the direct taxes falling on those who use objects of luxury. What has been said upon the indirect taxes on luxuries, will materially shorten our task.

This class comprehends a considerable portion of what in the English system of finance are called the assessed taxes, such as those on horses kept for pleasure, windows when more numerous or larger than required for health and comfort. Servants, except shopmen &c, hair powder, armorial bearings, carriages, game duty &c &c.

The motive for their establishment has been chiefly to increase the revenue, but in some degree perhaps to prevent unproductive expenditure, and to stimulate accumulation. Like ordinary taxes on luxuries they fall wholly on consumers, and are finally paid out of profits, rent and fixed incomes according to the class of society to which the individual originally defraying them belongs, but they have no tendency to diminish the general rate of either.

These taxes, being levied according to a return for the previous year, taken as a whole, are computable. They are however complex, their collection puts in motion a cumbrous machinery on the part of the Government and requires many troublesome acts on the part of the payers.

The land and assessed taxes which comprehend the great number of those we are now examining were collected in 1831 at an expense of about $5\frac{1}{3}$ per cent, being less than the cost of the customs or excise.[1] If however we consider that the last yield many times the amount of the first, and that the machinery employed in exacting an impost, by no means increases in proportion to the money amount levied by its means, we shall perhaps think that ceteris paribus direct taxes on luxuries are to be numbered among the frugal sources of revenue.

They are inconstant and indivisible on the whole. Still owing to the previous returns it is possible to calculate exactly what they will produce sometime beforehand. No plan has however been devised by means of which the legislator can either increase or diminish the amount they will furnish hereafter so as exactly to suit his wants. They might greatly gain in these qualities, as well as in that of computability, if those returns were to be made every year at the commencement of the parliamentary session of the amount of taxable objects existing in the country, and the tax be then assessed with a view to these returns.

These taxes must be considered popular, they fall on a few persons all

---

[1] [See Marshall op. cit. p. 21. In 1831 the gross revenue of the land and assessed taxes was £5,325,759 and the cost of collection was £282,337 or 5.3 per cent. For figures of 7.1 per cent for Customs and 6.7 for Excise, see notes on pp. 98, 103.]

belonging to the very richest class and even such may escape the payment, if they think fit, by abstaining from the use of the taxed articles.

They are but slightly interferent. they occasion little misapplication of productive industry. Should they be so heavy as to diminish the demand for a given article, the capital and labor previously employed in preparing it can be usually transferred to the production of some other, which will yield an almost equal profit. The national wealth then is only diminished by the sum which the tax produces except that at its first imposition some loss will probably occur before the transfer to a different employment is complete, which ought not to be wholly lost sight of.

These taxes are very unequal; one man may derive great enjoyment from the use of a carriage, which may indeed be necessary for his health; while another of equal fortune may prefer the exercise of walking or riding on horseback, in this case then, a tax on carriages would diminish the enjoyments of the first but not of the second. This example represents a numerous class, all of which sin against the just and plain rule, that a tax should deduct nearly a proportionate share of happiness from every class and individual possessing wealth in the community.

The tax on servants particularly presses on laborers in consequence of the motive it affords to the rich, to spend their money upon fine clothes or costly furniture in lieu of giving employment to labor. This proposition is proved by Mr Ricardo.[2]

They are not corruptive, nobody has any motive to elude them, except those who are finally called upon to pay them, nor do they hold out any considerable temptation to the abstinence from useful, or performance of hurtful actions.

They are vexatious and entail a great expenditure of time and trouble on

---

[2] [D. Ricardo *On the Principles of Political Economy and Taxation* ed. P. Sraffa, Cambridge: Cambridge University Press, 1951 pp. 392-394. Ricardo does not, however, consider explicitly the question of taxing servants.]

those who are subject to them, from the necessity of making complicated returns, which whether accurate or not, constantly produce surcharges. Then follow appeals, and a whole tribe of annoyances, comprehending a very disagreeable and inquisitorial inspection on the part of the agents of Government.

In point of evasibility the direct taxes on luxuries are far superior to any we have as yet criticized, and looking at them on the whole, we must consider them less pernicious than any source of revenue which contributes to fill the English exchequer, with the exception perhaps of the land tax.

Chapter 21

Taxes on Travelling and the Conveyance of Intelligence

The taxes which afford the subject of the present chapter, form the first of a whole family, which from their pernicious consequences, particularly merit the reprobation of those who have the welfare of mankind at heart. The qualities which peculiarly mark them are inequality and corruptiveness. They comprehend the imposts which have been laid on stage coaches, hackney coaches, and also the profits derived from the conveyance of letters. All fall upon those who take advantage of these several conveniences, with a few exceptions such as mercantile letters and parcels, which the reader will readily make for himself. The motive for their establishment has been usually legitimate; vizt. a wish to increase the revenue.[1]

---

[1][Marshall op. cit. pp. 16-19 provides figures for these taxes. The duty on post horses in 1831 raised £231,683. That on stage coaches produced £422,543. Statement III gives a figure of £71,153 for the combined duty on hackney coaches and hawkers. There does not seem to be a separate figure for hackney coaches.

The gross receipts from the postal duties were as follows: England inland, £1,695,737, twopenny £103,134, foreign £60,777; Scotland £204,693, Ireland £256,977. The total of £2,321,312 (Marshall, p. 19, lines 7-12) was thus substantial, and the costs imposed on communications correspondingly large. The system was however also charged with making postal deliveries and was criticised by contemporaries as inefficient and expensive to operate (Parnell, op. cit., pp. 117-118). Net payments into the Exchequer in 1831 were £1,391,006 for Great Britain, and £139,200 for Ireland (Marshall, p. 19, lines 50-51), making a total of £1,530,206. The net tax raised was thus only two thirds of the gross revenue, though it still contributed handsomely to the Exchequer. There are minor discrepancies in the figures: Statement III, line 5, of Marshall records a gross revenue for

They are all incomputable, inconstant, and indivisible. Nobody can tell what they will produce individually or collectively, nor on whom they will fall, nor is it possible to augment or lessen the revenue they yield, as the wants of the State may require. Their produce is moreover likely to vary greatly, from the influence of various accidental circumstances.

On the other hand, the possession of simplicity must be awarded to them; the acts involved in their collection are few and easy.

In point of frugality they differ, but it has been impossible to ascertain what percentage each of them costs in collection. The post house duty is farmed, had it remained in the hands of the Government, it is probable that a separate board would have been created for its management with a whole tribe of subordinate officers to perform the duty, which is now so well performed by the keepers of turnpike gates. The old hackney coach board, a case in point could be considered in no other light than a gross job.

The sum paid for the conveyance of letters in 1831 was about £2,500,000 and the net revenue about £1,530,000, but it would be unfair to reckon the whole of the difference between these two sums or indeed a large proportion of it, as the expense of collection. Were the tax abolished, it would still be necessary to convey letters, at a cost, probably little inferior to what is now paid. The collection of the impost can add but little to the disbursements.

Taxes on travelling and on the conveyance of intelligence are not unpopular owing to their comparatively small amount, the large number of persons,

the Post Office in 1831 of £2,184,000 for Great Britain alone (compared with £2,064,341 above), and Statement IV line 6 records £1,989,295 for the UK as a whole in 1831. Marshall p. 23 line 14 gives the cost of transport of post as £320,305 for the UK. Deducting this from the gross receipts for the UK of £2,321,312 leaves £2,001,007 which, compared with net tax receipts of £1,530,206 leaves £470,801 to be accounted for. From Marshall, pp. 18-19, lines 40-49, charges for such items as 'incidents', pensions, salaries and allowances total £249,143. The discrepancy between this and £470,801 raises further questions about the position of the Post Office as a branch of the tax system, given the contemporary habit of disbursements from public revenues, for associates. On the postal duties and the introduction of the Penny Post in 1839 see McCulloch op. cit. Part II, Chapter VII, pp. 310-323. McCulloch was fiercely critical of the introduction of the Penny Post and the abandonment of postal charges as a source of tax revenue (ibid. p. 321).]

by whom they are finally paid, and the ignorance that prevails as to their real effects. Added to this they are so confounded, with the objects with which they are associated as in some degree to escape the public eye, and lose their real character.

We may venture to predict that before many years are over, their popularity will cease, that desirable end will be attained when the people shall perceive that the greatest ingenuity could hardly have devised a method of levying the small sum they yield in a way more hostile to the general improvement and happiness.

They are very interferent. Nobody can doubt this who believes that the beneficial employment of capital and labour is promoted by travelling and epistolary correspondence, and that advantageous speculations would be undertaken, were it not for the obstacles which they impose. In this respect they diminish the national wealth to a greater extent, than could be done by their mere money amount, supposing that amount to be levied in some other way.

They are very unequal. An equal tax should deduct a similar proportionate share of enjoyment from each person possessing wealth in the community. Can this be said of the revenue derived from the post office, or levied in different shapes from travellers? Most certainly not. These fall chiefly on the active, the intelligent and well-informed, while the slothful, the ignorant, and the stupid, are comparatively freed from their grasp. So far from making a claim on the subject in proportion to his wealth, they almost pass over the most opulent class, and impose a severe burden on those who are least able to bear it. In many instances perhaps they wholly interrupt all communication between the members of indigent families, whom the necessity of gaining a hardly earned subsistence has widely dispersed, and thus interfere with the natural affections and sympathies.

The corruptiveness of these taxes deserves peculiar attention, and has been already alluded to. It is desirable to enlarge a little upon it here, even at the risk of repeating what was said about that quality in the last section. They act corruptively, not when they are paid, but when they are not paid, when they prevent the performance of useful actions, and yield nothing to the State. The advantage obtained by the State from the payment of a tax, is simply derived from the power of purchasing possessed by the sum paid into the exchequer. The Government should endeavour to obtain this power in the simplest possible manner. It can gain nothing, but on the contrary must lose, if it holds out to the subject the least unnecessary inducement to abstain from any acts, which may lead to his moral, intellectual, or physical improvement. Nor can any body doubt but that travelling and letter writing are eminently beneficial, that they enlarge the mind, stimulate its faculties, afford a necessary help to traffic, invigorate the health, or at least yield an innocent pleasure?

If we examine the situation of countries whose inhabitants are comparatively deprived of their advantages, we shall find them generally slothful and ignorant, and we may even form an estimate of the moral condition of a Nation, as soon as we know whether the individuals composing it are fond of travelling, and epistolary correspondence or otherwise. Thus the Anglo-Americans are perhaps the greatest travellers, the English come next, and the people of Europe follow, nearly in the order of their relative civilization.

Mankind are often cheated by names. The fines imposed by the judge on those who transgress the law differ but in name from the taxes we are now examining.[2]

Let us then drop the word tax, and use that of penalty instead. Is there any body bold enough to say that it is wise and just in the legislature, to impose a penalty however inconsiderable upon each person who travels in a stage coach or receives a letter? When will the common sense of the world

---

[2] [Manuscript note, possibly by G. Grote] Why is the term Penalty more applicable to this than to many other cases? The assessed taxes for instance. The penalty upon living in a house, upon riding a horse, &c &c.

revolt at such absurdity? It may perhaps be said even granting the principles laid down, that the evil created by the taxes now under consideration is very small. That almost as many letters are written now, as would be written, in case the post office charges should be reduced, so as barely to pay its expenses. Those who argue thus must be prepared to maintain that the mails would be no more loaded than they are, were their contents to be transmitted to all parts of the empire free of all charge. The striking difference in the numbers who pass over a bridge, where a toll is paid, and another where nothing is demanded from the passengers might teach them their mistake. Postage is a heavy disbursement to a poor man.

We may here observe that the conveyance of letters is one of the few enterprises possessing at all a commercial character, which a Government ought to undertake, instead of leaving it to private individuals. In everything relating to it, the strictest economy should be used; the demand made should never exceed the charges incurred, and it may even be doubted, whether letters should not be conveyed free of expense, as is now done with newspapers.

Were the post-office abandoned to individual enterprise, the communication between large towns would probably be cheaper, more expeditious and as secure as at present; but small towns and villages would hardly pay for the advantages they now enjoy in this respect, and there would be a want of combination in the general arrangements.

The public does not consider these imposts vexatious, and we cannot venture to call them so. Under the head of evasibility, the only one open to objection is that on letters.

Chapter 22

Taxes on Justice

We have now reached the most pernicious means that have ever been invented for rendering a portion of the National wealth subservient to the purposes of Government, without actual violence. In civilized countries, where the state of opinion and of manners forbids the bare-faced robberies of the Satrap and Pasha, no source of revenue ranks so low as law taxes.

Taxes on justice! Premiums to injustice! What terms of reprobation can more strongly point their direct opposition to all the ends for which mankind submit to the bonds of political union.

The following are the principal imposts which form the subject of the present chapter.

1. Stamps on all instruments required in suits at law

2. Fees paid in Courts of Justice

3. Fees on the enrollment of Attorneys, Advocates &c mentioned in the chapter 19.

The second class is even more pernicious than the first although not usually paid at once to the State, but to certain officers of the courts; because while the fees are employed to reward public services, they create in those who receive them a strong motive to extend and perpetuate abuses.

Law taxes fall wholly on those who first pay them, on litigants. These individuals do not possess the power of shifting the load from their own shoulders, except perhaps in a few rare cases. The motive for the establishment of stamps has been wholly to augment the revenue. Fees have usually taken their origin in the unauthorized exactions of those intrusted with the administration of justice, and have been afterwards either openly or tacitly confirmed, by the legislative authority. They add one to the numberless proofs, that man will usually employ irresponsible power for his own ends, regardless of the sufferings of others.

What has been said on travelling &c in the chapter 21, applies in so many respects to law taxes, that it is only necessary to say that they are incomputable inconstant and indivisible.

On the other hand they possess simplicity and frugality. The stamps taken altogether cost in Great Britain in 1831 only about £1.8.0 per cent.[1]

They are also upon the whole popular and unevasible.

The deep and unanswerable objections to them will appear, by examining them strictly with reference to the other desirable qualities.

They are very interferent; although it is difficult to compute the exact

---

[1] [It is not clear how Norman calculated a figure of 1.4 per cent (one pound, eight shillings per cent). Marshall, op. cit., p. 17, line 1, gives the proceeds of law taxes as £1,412,553 for 1831, excluding those on legacies, line 2 (£1,144,459) and probates, line 3, (£876,939) which are discussed separately by Norman in chapter 27. The total proceeds from all the 'assessed' taxes, was £6,945,559. But the total was made up by the proceeds from a number of other duties, discussed by Norman in separate chapters, including bills of exchange, receipts and advertisements (chapter 23), post horses (chapter 21), and cards and dice (chapter 30). Taking law taxes alone, the costs of collection, calculated from 13 items under this head on pp. 16-17 was, at £154,239, 10.9 per cent of the duty. If legacy and probate duties are included, the collection cost falls to 4.49 per cent. But even if all the assessed taxes are included, the collection cost comes to 2.2 per cent of the revenue. *Parliamentary Papers* 1824 (69) XVII p. 483 shows the expenses of the legacy duty office as £4,954 and the proceeds of the tax for the following year as £1,801,841. This gives a cost ratio of only 0.28 per cent. But the precise basis of the figures used by different authorities is not always clear; Marshall op. cit. p. 17 line 2 reports the proceeds of the legacy duty for 1824 as only £1,049,458, or little more than half the figure above. As McCulloch pointed out, the taxes on successions and legacies involved no less than three different taxes (*Treatise on the Principles and Practical Influence of Taxation and the Funding System*, 1st edition, London: Longman, 1845 p. 290).]

effect of the denial of justice, caused by the law taxes, upon the free distribution of industry in such a country as Great Britain. Yet that the diminution of wealth it occasions is great, may be shewn by observing countries, in which the same effect takes place from a similar cause still more violent in its operation.

Spain, Barbary, parts of Italy, and Turkey are blessed with a soil and climate far more prolific, in the most valuable natural productions, far better adapted to the growth of some manufacturers, than these our northern regions, yet they are all poor, the insecurity of property removes the great stimulus to industry. Who will labor to produce that of which the hand of violence may speedily bereave him?

In the favored regions of the South, other causes certainly aid in the lamentable result we see, but to the prevailing insecurity of property, we must attribute the largest portion of the evil. In Great Britain the law taxes, frequently occasioning as they do a denial of justice, must create a degree of insecurity, which though less pernicious than that arising from open violence, possesses the same tendency, and must produce a similar effect. We may then feel confident that great good would result from the abolition of these pernicious imposts, from the more advantageous direction given to the capital and labor of the Nation. It may also be remarked though the observation hardly falls within the scope of this essay, that a similar end would be attained, by introducing into our jurisprudence, those ameliorations, for which enlightened men have been so long striking.

Law taxes are grossly and palpably unequal. We have seen that they fall almost wholly on those who first pay them; on litigants, half of whom have suffered a wrong and can only obtain redress through the courts, or who will suffer a wrong unless the judicature protects them in the enjoyment of their rights. Eventually indeed these persons may perhaps, (supposing them to possess the means of making the first outlay) recover a part of what they have so paid, from the offending party, but in many cases, the expenses of legal process are so great as to secure injustice a complete impunity. Those who have been injured must be able to make the first advance; this is a necessary condition for the obtaining relief. The greater the amount of wrong they have sustained, the less will be their ability to do so. Dishonesty and fraud, will ever have reason to rejoice at the existence of law taxes, for these are their protectors, their guardians, their friends. At the present day the far larger part of the British nation, are almost excluded, by their influence in a great degree, though other abuses contribute to the effect, from redress in all civil wrongs. Of the 24 millions who form our population it is not too much to affirm that 18 millions are unable to defray the costs of an action in any tribunal, but a Court of Requests. But some will say, why all this noise about stamps and fees, which seldom exceed a few pounds, and often only amount to a few shillings? Why? Because a sum of money is large or small relatively to the wealth which a man possesses. The laborer who has nothing but his daily earnings say at the rate of 10s per week, endures as much if he be deprived of 10s as the Duke with £50,000 per annum suffers from the loss of £1,000.

A good taxation should take from all possessing property an equal proportion of that property. The law taxes fasten on those who have suffered a wrong, who have peculiar claims for forbearance, and leave their fortunate neighbours untouched. Even among their victims, they make no allowance for differences of fortune. They may deprive a man of £100 because he cannot advance £1 or £2. Can inequality go farther?

Law taxes are corruptive in a very high degree, narrowing, or wholly closing the doors of the tribunals. They contain in their very nature a direct invitation to the foulest wickedness. Oppression, fraud, malice, and revenge follow in their train, and while gorging themselves with unhallowed spoils, laugh at that empty apparel of justice which they so well know can seldom drive them from their prey. Whatever evils judicial establishments are calculated when properly administered to prevent, must of course be encouraged by law taxes. The great end of Government is security, the protection of the weak against the oppressions of the strong. The giving an overwhelming motive to each individual so to shape his actions, that they may not inflict injury upon others, while at the same time he feels assured, that he shall never be thwarted in the employment of his means, for those legal purposes, which he may judge most conducive to his happiness. Now to security. Law taxes are essentially opposed. Being direct impediments to the execution of the law, they tend to encourage that line of conduct, which the law, was it not thus impeded, would more or less perfectly prevent. Could the votes of all thieves and rogues be taken on the question of their abolition, they would unanimously decide in the negative. We need not point out what should be the vote of honest men.

The following would be a proper preamble to any act of Parliament, increasing the amount of stamps on law proceedings, or the fees paid to officers of the courts,

> Whereas it appears that many persons who have defrauded their neighbours and have committed deeds of oppression and cruelty, have been prosecuted and brought to punishment, notwithstanding the many existing statutes creating heavy law taxes. And whereas it is highly desirable that such persons should not be molested in future, but should be left in the free enjoyment of the riches, possessions and titles they may have thus acquired, may it please your majesty &c &c.

Law taxes may often occasion great annoyances, trouble and loss of time and money, to those who are called upon to pay them, and are therefore vexatious.

This chapter may be closed with a remark which we have often had occasion to make previously, though with a different application. Whenever the expense of litigation is such as to prevent a person, who has suffered a wrong, from making any appeal to the laws, the revenue gains nothing. Therefore, in such a case the suffering of innocence, the triumph of crime, and the long train of evil consequences likely to arise in the way of example, are all so much mischief, uncompensated by the addition of even one farthing to the exchequer. It is only when the injustice is less complete, when the sufferer possesses the means to enter a court of judicature, that the mass of evil created is balanced by even the most inconsiderable portion of good.

Chapter 23

Taxes on the Transfer of Property, on Knowledge, on Prudence, on Ingenuity, and on Health

The minuteness with which the taxes lately commented on have been examined, will enable us to discuss more succinctly the remainder of what may be called par excellence, the corruptive and interferent taxes. These may be arranged in five groups:

1. Taxes on the transfer of property

2. Taxes on knowledge

3. Taxes on prudence

4. Taxes on ingenuity

5. Taxes on health

The chief object in the establishment of all, has been the augmentation of the revenue. Though a desire in one portion of the governing body to diminish the circulation of newspapers by increasing their price, and the interests of existing journalists and practitioners to uphold a system which creates a virtual monopoly in their favor have also produced some effect.

Commercial stamps usually augment the costs of production, and fall on the consumers of the articles to which they apply, the remainder of the first group fall generally on the seller.

Taxes on knowledge are paid by the purchasers of paper, books, and newspapers.

Taxes on prudence, excepting those on commercial risks, fall on persons making insurances.

Taxes on ingenuity [fall] on the ingenious in the first instance at least. Those on health, upon professional aspirants, or on the sick.

Taken as a whole, all must be considered incomputable, inconstant and indivisible. On the other hand they are simple frugal and inevasible and, with some diffidence, we may pronounce them to be, compared with many other imposts, popular and unvexatious.

It is true that lately a good many petitions have been presented to Parliament against the taxes on knowledge, but these have been chiefly originated by a few active and enlightened men; the middle orders generally speaking, have remained passive, unaware of the evil inflicted on them.

The first group, and to a certain extent the second, third and fourth are interferent; they prevent the free development of industry, and throw an obstacle in the way of the best possible distribution of capital, labor and land. This is obvious, for suppose that A wishes to sell a farm to B but is prevented by the expense attending a transfer, and that B is willing to purchase were that impediment not in the way, it may be safely assumed, that a better distribution of property than that which now exists is prevented from taking place. The very desire of A to possess the money rather than the land almost proves that he can make more of it; that it is more valuable to him, while the wish of B to possess the land rather than the money, evinces that he can employ the latter more advantageously than the former.

This inference flows naturally from the fundamental principle that the majority of men in such matters are the best judges of their own interests.

Generalising from the above example, it seems clear that evil must flow from anything which has a tendency to prevent or impede the operations of the purchaser and seller.

Again A would employ a certain sum in paying B to insure his property did not the tax prevent him, or would be aware of the advantages arising from insurance was he not prevented from acquiring knowledge by the high price of books &c arising from taxation.

Policy duties on marine Insurances, are rapidly driving away from England a profitable branch of commerce, and the same thing is threatened with regard to land insurances. The French fire offices have established agencies in London, and will find means to transact business in spite of legal obstacles; a difference in expense of more than 100 per cent is sure to attract customers and sharpen ingenuity.

The imposts now under consideration are unequal in a high degree; the circumstances that make them so, have been well explained by A. Smith. As far as the first group is concerned he says 'taxes on the sale of land', and he might have added most of those paid on the transfer of property, 'fall altogether on the seller. The seller is almost always under the necessity of selling, and must therefore take what he can get. The buyer is scarce ever under the necessity of buying, and will therefore only give such a price as he likes. He considers what the Land will cost him in tax and price altogether. The more he is obliged to pay in the way of tax, the less he will be disposed to give in the way of price. Such taxes fall almost always on a necessitous person and must therefore be very cruel and oppressive.'[1]

---

[1] [Adam Smith *An Inquiry into the Nature and Causes of the Wealth of Nations* (1776) ed. E. Cannan, London, 1904, reprinted London: Methuen, 1961, Book V, Chapter II, Arts I and II Appendix, p. 390. 'Taxes upon the sale of land fall altogether upon the seller. The seller is almost always under the necessity of selling, and must, therefore, take such a price as he can get. The buyer is scarce ever under the necessity of buying, and

Those on knowledge and prudence fall wholly on the consumer, except
when they have a purely commercial character, and thus are chiefly paid by
the wisest and most virtuous portion of the community.

The excessive corruptiveness of these taxes is however their worst feature.
The second, third, fourth and fifth groups almost all act as penalties on
the performance of virtuous or useful and therefore praise-worthy actions,
they hold out an inducement, an invitation to abstain from these, and in
many cases produce the effect of preventing them, without any benefit to the
revenue. It would be desirable to make a calculation of the extent to which
they thus operate, but on this point no certainty can be obtained. However
the difference between Great Britain and the United States, with respect to
the number of advertisements, may enable us to form a guess.

It is stated by Sir H. Parnell that there are annually 963,000 in the former
and ten millions in the latter.[2]

Was it not for the stamp duties on insurances, it is probable that the
owners of hardly any property exposed to the danger of fire would omit to
secure themselves against its ravages. Yet we know that a large proportion
is not insured at all, and much of the remainder for less than its value. The
enormous duty of 2s/6d while the premium is generally only 1s/6d is the
obstacle. Was this removed insurances against fire would be universal, and
conflagrations would almost cease to be an evil. For the offices would make
their calculations, so as just to leave a moderate profit for the shareholders,
and the general loss being paid by the whole body of insurers would fall so
lightly as to be hardly sensible.

---

will, therefore, only give such a price as he likes. He considers what the land will cost him
in tax and price together. The more he is obliged to pay in the way of tax, the less he will
be disposed to give in the way of price. Such taxes, therefore, fall almost always upon a
necessitous person, and must, therefore, be frequently very cruel and oppressive.']

[2]Sir H. Parnell on Fin. Reform p.41. [This was not in the first (1830) edition of Parnell.
See however the third (1831) edition, pp. 43-4.]

It may here be observed that the want of a general registration, and the barbarous system of conveyancing which is substituted for it in England, creates a heavy tax upon property, the produce of which goes not to the public revenue, but to the lawyers. That it should be allowed to continue, is a striking proof of how short a distance we have yet advanced in the career of civilization.

Chapter 24

Taxes on Rent, Tythe, Land Tax

We have now arrived at a class of taxes, which in many respects are preferable to any others; and which when less worthy of praise, owe their faults to some errors in the mode of levying them, or of applying their produce, by no means necessarily belonging to them. The first to be examined is Tithe. So numerous and contradictory have been the opinions expressed by different authors, upon the nature and effect of this impost, that it becomes expedient to examine its mode of operation at somewhat greater length than has been required in the preceding part of this section. Still this must be done succinctly; for so much might be said upon it even without attempting to exhaust the subject as to form alone an extensive treatise. All that will be now attempted, is to give such an analysis of a somewhat difficult matter as can be afforded in a few pages, without pretending to answer all the objections that an ingenious disputant might raise.

In England about $\frac{1}{3}$rd of the land is either Tithe free or subject to a modus,[1] and in the remaining $\frac{2}{3}$rds a composition commonly exists, in the shape of a money payment below the real value. In what follows these circumstances which do not affect the principle of the tax will be disregarded

---

[1] [Money payment in lieu of tithe.]

in order to simplify the subject, and confine it within manageable limits.

Tithe in an old country is a tax on rent. To understand the nature of a tax on rent it is necessary to form a clear idea of rent itself. This point then must be first considered.

Land, being of limited extent its owners are able to obtain for its produce under favorable circumstances a greater price than would be necessary to repay the labor and capital employed upon it with a reasonable profit. The excess is rent. This excess might exist even if all the land in a country was of the same degree of fertility and possessed the same advantages in point of situation, roads, markets &c, but speaking practically, this assumed equality never occurs. In every country the gradations in soil and the necessary conveniences are numerous, and even in the richest and best tilled, there are usually some lands, which remain unoccupied because they will not repay the mere expense of cultivation. In every country also there are portions of which the crops will only just give a return for the capital employed, without yielding any rent, and the difference in amount of produce from this, the worst land in cultivation, after the expenditure of a given amount of capital, and that of any superior land, is the measure of the rent paid for the latter.

In the progress of society rent commences within a short period after land has been appropriated, and has a constant tendency to increase with the progress of population and wealth. The process is as follows. As the inhabitants become more numerous, a constantly increasing supply of food and raw produce is required. The price therefore rises, and with each rise in price, it becomes profitable to have recourse to a kind of land of inferior quality, and situation, to that which had been previously occupied, or to expend more capital on the old land with a less return. When one step in the scale has been taken, it is equally advantageous to pay a rent for the superior soils, or to have the worst for nothing, and under such circumstances, rent will and indeed must be paid. The competition of capitalists, and the general equalization of profits arising from it, renders this result necessary and unavoidable.

Supposing for a moment that no corn can be imported: the quantity and price of the grain produced will depend upon the number and condition of the people, including in the latter item, the price they are able and willing to pay for food. If they are able and willing for instance to pay 50s per quarter for wheat, land will be cultivated on which that grain can be grown, so as to be sold at 50s without leaving any surplus, consequently without paying any rent. It is obvious from this, that rent in its simple form cannot enter into price.

Having got so far we are now in a condition to explain the nature of Tithe.

The great and marked distinction between Tithe and ordinary rent, consists in the circumstance, that the former is taken from that land which pays no rent, in the common acceptation of the term – that it is a portion of the gross produce, instead of the surplus remaining after the expense of cultivation has been paid – and our object now is, to shew that notwithstanding this apparent dissimilarity, in a country like England, tithe nevertheless is a part of rent, that it has not raised prices, and thus fallen on the consumer, but that it has simply diminished the income of the landowner. This it accomplishes by preventing a descent into inferior soils, or an application of more capital to old lands, with a smaller return. Without it worse land would have been about what it is now, and the Tithe now paid on inferior soils yielding no rent, would have become rent, and as such passed into the hands of the landowners. In order to subscribe to this view of the subject, it is especially necessary to keep in mind that population will always press upon the means of support.

Tithe is one tenth of the gross produce of the land. The cultivator pays the expense of producing the 10/10ths, and only receives 9/10ths the effect to him and to the country is the same as if the soil was rendered sterile to that extent. In the progress of cultivation Tithe must have first fallen on the consumer; it must then, when rent would otherwise have appeared, have fallen partly on the consumer and partly on the landowner, and finally when and where in the natural course of things rent would have exceeded 1/10th of the gross produce, it must have been wholly transferred to the latter. It is peculiarly necessary to mark here the sequence of events, population increases, the nation requires more corn, and is able and willing to pay an increased price for it, the price rises, new land is taken into cultivation on which corn can be raised at that price without rent. The price it must be recollected does not advance because worse land is tilled, but worse land is tilled because the price has risen. Tithe if it exists does not raise the price, but arrests the cultivation at a better quality of land, than would otherwise be cultivated, at a quality which will yield corn at the assumed price, after paying this form of rent.

Suppose Tithe to be abolished tomorrow, what would be the consequence? Prices would fall for a time, because the cultivation would obtain 10/10ths for what the 9/10ths now cost him, and would extend his operations. Production would thus increase, and with the falling prices an impulse be given to population, which would increase, until corn raised on the worst land in cultivation minus the tithe, cost as much as that raised on the worst tithed land cost previously. The cycle would then be complete, prices would be as before, and the ultimate result would be to give landlords the whole of the Tithe minus the sum expended on inferior soils in the shape of increased rent, while the quantity of corn grown, and the population would both have augmented an imposition of tithe, where none previously existed, would stop or retard the progress of population, a part of the land would be thrown out of cultivation and less corn would be produced, until it had fixed, after a temporary rise, at the previous price, or at the price at which it would then have been, had Tithe continued to exist, when the whole amount of the burden would be fixed on the landowners. In both cases a generation or two at most would suffice to produce the effect.

Such is the state of things where rent exists and where the Tithe is less in value than the rent. In a country where there should be no rent, Tithe still acting as if it occasioned sterility in the soil, to the extent of causing a diminution of 1/10th in the produce would fall on consumers, would raise prices, and retard the increase of population, and the period when rent would be paid.

The payment of Tithe in kind is to be attributed chiefly to the early period of its establishment when money payments were little known, and to its having subsequently belonged to a corporation, ill-disposed to change both from interest and habit. Rent in former times was generally paid in kind here, and continues to be so, in many parts of France, Italy and other continental countries at the present day.

The views here exhibited are opposed to the prevailing popular opinions. It is usually assumed, that the Tithe in this country falls either on farmers or on consumers; and hence the cry for its abolition. If however it be true, that prices would have been as high at the present moment, as they now are, had Tithe never existed, it is clear that both these opinions must be as incorrect as they are interdestructive. The former can be readily shewn to be without foundation, by a very simple and easy argument. Farmers are capitalists. They are manufacturers of raw produce. The tendency to an equalization in profits renders it absurd to imagine, that they can obtain, all things taken into account, a less return for their capitals than other producers. In making a bargain for a farm, they calculate before hand all the burdens in Tithe taxes rates &c, and only covenant to pay to the landlord, that portion of the surplus which remains. To suppose that they calculate otherwise, would be to accuse them of insanity.

But if all this be true it may be asked, why then is Tithe the object of such general dislike? Why is it detested, while the land tax a sister impost, has never been selected for abolition by the most furious demagogue? The answer is obvious. The phenomenon is to be ascribed:

1. To the application of Tithe

2. To the mode of collection and to the circumstance that an abolition of
   Tithe would obviously be followed in the first instance by increased cultivation, and a fall in the price of agricultural produce, which would not
   be the case with the abolition of a land tax. The first being an anticipation of rent, when rent would otherwise exist, the latter a payment
   out of rent already existing.

A discussion on the first point, however interesting lies beyond the limits
of this work; the latter will be adverted to, in our examination of the extent
to which Tithe possesses the desirable qualities. To this examination we now
proceed.

Tithe as at present collected is incomputable, inconstant and indivisible,
though in all these points, it would admit of easy amendment, through the
medium of a commutation. It is also highly prodigal. In most parishes, when
taken in kind, the expense of collection averages perhaps 20 per cent of the
value. Wagons and men must be sent into almost every field, a part of each
load is taken in one place, a part in another, and the whole must be brought
to one or more homesteads, usually at a considerable distance. The quality
of the Tithed produce is generally indifferent. In harvesting it, advantage
cannot be taken of favorable weather, and the result is, that a great deal
suffers from exposure.

The extreme unpopularity of Tithe has already been adverted to, and
requires no further explanation.

It is interferent. More capital would be employed on the land were it
abolished, and the general system of husbandry would perhaps be better.[2]

Tithe cannot be considered corruptive, except in so far, as it places the
pastor and his flock in an insidious and inconvenient relation to each other.

---

[2] [Ms note, probably in the hand of George Grote] Query this – More capital would be
employed but not with a greater return.

In this point of view indeed, nothing can be conceived more absurd and irrational, than the present mode of levying Tithe. Instead of being collected directly from the landowner who really pays it, the impost is demanded in the first instance from the occupier, and a mass of evil passions are generated between persons who for the good of society ought to regard each other with no other feelings than those of respect, confidence, and love.

Tithe even in its present state can hardly be called a very unequal tax though it varies so much in amount in different districts, and even in neighbouring parishes; because these differences have usually been allowed for in bequests, sales and leases, a purchaser or renter of land knows that he only contracts for the net produce, after 1/10th of the gross produce has been deducted, and cannot therefore complain of injustice. A new and first tax on rent would of course be unequal unless balanced by an equivalent impost, on capitalists or annuitants. However it may be allowed that owing to the different dispositions and tastes of successive incumbents and lay impropriators, some objection may fairly be urged against Tithe, as it present exists, under this head, though to a less extent than is commonly imagined.

Tithe, as now collected is usually vexatious; in this respect perhaps no impost is equally objectionable. It would seem that the most perverse ingenuity had been employed to make it a source of trouble and annoyance. It is not at all evasible.

It now only remains that we should say a little upon the mode of retaining the good, and curing the evil of Tithe. To abolish it altogether, as proposed by some well meaning persons, would be to abandon an excellent source of revenue, and to hand over a tax which has existed for seven or eight centuries, and which in every point of view must be considered national property, to the present race of landowners who have no more equitable claim to it, than on any other section of the community. A commutation for a corn rent assessed on occupiers during the currency of existing leases, and on owners afterwards, is the obvious course to adopt. The rate of commutation might be reviewed from time to time. The periods of any one arrangement, in that case, ought to extend over such a number of years, as would tend to equalize the variety of seasons. Experience shows that about 20 years would be required for this purpose; or an arrangement might be made once for all. This would save future trouble and expense, but would be liable to the objection of being at first perhaps too unfavorable and afterwards too favorable to landowners, in consequence of the immediate fall, and ultimate probable advance in the price of raw produce owing to the increase in the Population and wealth &c of the country. Even a free trade in all agricultural commodities might check, but would not destroy this last tendency. It is obviously impossible in this work, to enter into the detail of a plan of commutation, and it must suffice to conclude, by stating, that a well-devised scheme would at once remove all the objections against Tithe, and would render it computable, simple, constant, divisible, popular, and unvexatious. This impost would then possess all the qualities it at present wants, and would nearly resemble the land tax.

After what has been said it is unnecessary to enlarge upon the nature and properties of the land tax. The reader will readily perceive that it possess all the desirable qualities. In England though irregular it is not even unequal, because the apparent irregularities which at first made it so, have been corrected or allowed for, by a long series of purchases and descents. When newly established, it would require to render it equal, an equivalent tax on other kinds of property. It is bitterly to be lamented that the land tax when first established in the reign of William III, had not been fairly assessed over the whole country, and declared to be a permanent charge to the extent of 4s in the pound on the rental. Had this been done, the revenue would now receive perhaps 8 millions a year from the most unexceptionable of all sources, the burden would be felt by nobody, and a whole host of impolitic taxes would be rendered unnecessary.

Chapter 25

Continuation of Taxes on Rent, Poor Rate, House and Window Tax

The most interesting question that suggests itself upon an examination of the poor rate, is that which relates to their tendency. Does their existence on the whole produce good or evil? But the discussion to which this question would give rise lies beyond the limit of our subject. Nothing need be said as to the intention of the legislature which established a poor rate.

Both it and the taxes enumerated after it fell in by far the larger proportion upon the proprietors of fixed property in general. Thus constituting a tax upon rent, not merely rent peculiarly and technically so called, which is derived from land mines &c and is alone subject to Tithe, but also on that species of it, which separated by an almost evanescent line, forms the profits of capital embarked in the building of houses, manufactories &c &c, a source of income which resembles in most of the phenomena attending it, including the important incident that it is the consequence and not the cause of price, the income of land and mine, owners and usually receives the same name.

It must be recollected that when capital has been thus embarked, it cannot in general be extricated, but remains indissolubly attached to the soil.

The poor rate being always confessedly and avowedly levied on the rental, we might refer to the chapter 24 wherein it has been shewn, that a tax on rent cannot be thrown upon any other source of income, and that thus the poor rate must be paid by the receivers of rent alone. However it will perhaps be expedient while directing the reader's attention to what has been already said, to enter a little into detail at present as respects not land but houses. The man who builds a house for sale or lease, acts like him who sows a field. He knows the price of the article he shall have to dispose of and calculates that it will repay his outlay. The only difference is that the former must expect to obtain a ground rent somewhat greater than the soil he intends to cover with brick and mortar would yield, if cultivated, and must recollect that his capital, if once embarked can never be recalled. Owing to this last circumstance and the comparatively long duration of the commodity produced the house market has and may be overstocked for a longer period than that of Mark Lane.

The sum paid by the occupier for the use of buildings may be generally divided into two parts:

1. The ground rent

2. The profit on the Capital Embarked

The first is rent in its strictest sense, it is the price paid for a monopoly, the owner of which has no power of procuring remuneration for any peculiar burden laid upon him, having already received all that the public is willing to give. This burden may be so great as to absorb his whole revenue, still he will be unable to throw any portion of it on other persons. The owner of the ground and the burden are like the landowner and farmer. The tax when imposed before the buildings are erected may be considered to fall upon the former, until the ground rent is exhausted, or until it is reduced to what the land would yield in rent if cultivated, beyond that point, it will put a stop to the speculation altogether or will fall upon the builder, supposing his capital to be already embarked. If however the ground rent should be more than absorbed by anticipation before the houses be built, and houses be still required, the excess of tax will fall on the consumers, that is the occupiers.

Thus one way in which the poor rates and similar taxes act upon the interests of the proprietors of land &c &c, is not so much to take away rent from them after it has been created as to prevent its creation.

This is easily shewn from observing the mode in which building speculations are carried on in London and its neighbourhood. The builder takes a lease of a portion of land for a long term, agreeing to pay for it a certain annual sum, during the currency of the lease, he thus becomes a proprietor, but should he perceive beforehand that the public burdens are likely to absorb more than the value of the monopoly, he will of course refrain from a losing operation. In this case the owner's loss exactly resembles that caused to the proprietor of the worst land in cultivation by the Tithe, which would be paid to him in the shape of rent, did not the impost prevent the descent into still worst soils.

The rent received by the builder, independent of the ground rent is not in the first instance the price paid for a monopoly, but a return for capital embarked, but when once his capital is invested, it cannot be withdrawn and his profit rent acquires all the essential properties of rent properly so called. He cannot compel the occupier to pay him more than the market price for his commodity notwithstanding an increase in the public burthens.

It may indeed happen that these public burthens may wholly absorb the ground rent, except a very inconsiderable portion. As has been already observed in this case only, were new houses required, would the price be regulated by the cost of building and the occupier be called upon to pay exactly what would afford fair return for it. Such probably is often the case with a certain description of badly situated houses even while those well placed are in great demand with high rents or prices. Situation and convenience with respect to houses stand in the relation of situation and fertility with respect to land.

It is obvious then on the whole that the occupier of a house, under ordinary circumstances, no more pays the taxes upon it, than a farmer those upon his farm. He calculates all his outgoings before he makes his bargain, and undertakes to pay accordingly.

The result of all this is that on houses about to be built the taxes now existing will fall on the groundowners, till the ground rent is absorbed. Beyond that if houses are still required on occupiers, but that new taxes on existing houses will fall wholly on their immediate proprietors whether free or lease-holders.

But to return from this discussion. The doctrine that the poor rate and similar imposts fall upon rent, is confirmed by uniform and frequent experience. In the parish of Cholesbury in Buckinghamshire the rates first ate up the whole rent, and afterwards touched upon the farmer's profits. So that at length nobody could be found to cultivate the land which was abandoned to the poor. A similar state of things is not infrequent in the South of England, with respect to isolated farms, and in one part of the country or another, cases may be found of every gradation between such as are last cited, and the enjoyment of a fair portion of the net produce of the land, by the proprietor, owing to his being subject to only a moderate share of public burdens.

In large towns such as London, where building speculations are carried on upon an extensive scale, a similar phenomenon occurs.

The house and window taxes precisely resemble the poor rate, except that the second is an impost on the enjoyment of light and therefore eminently corruptive.

The poor rate is, or might easily be rendered, by being imposed directly on the owner, computable, simple, frugal, constant, divisible, noninterferent, except when it absorbs more than the ground rent, and unevasible.

Popular and unvexatious as a tax can be, which raises above seven millions annually in England alone.

Uncorruptive, with reference to the mode of levying the money, though horribly the reverse with respect to its application, a matter which lies beyond the scope of this work.

The poor-rate must be considered unequal. Those who have either purchased or inherited land or houses, have certainly done so, knowing it was liable to the burden of maintaining the poor. But in many instances the increase had gone beyond all reasonable anticipation and leaves them in a far worse situation than they had any ground to expect.[1]

Another source of inequality arises from the circumstance, that the assessments are made, and the money levied, and in practice employed by the occupiers who while they do not really contribute any thing themselves being compensated by diminished rents, for whatever they apparently pay, often find their advantage, in a lavish expenditure, in the shape of low wages &c. It is true that low wages by their reaction increase the rent of land, in agricultural districts, so that there is sometimes a compensation to a certain extent in a round-about way but this does not reach the owners of isolated houses, or of houses in towns.

It would be an improvement in all these taxes to levy the tax from the proprietor, and not from the owner.

In the greater part of India and other Eastern countries the sovereign has always been considered the sole proprietor of the soil, and rent has defrayed the largest proportion of the public expenditure. Such is the case in our Asiatic empire where it has received the name of land revenue. It is administered under two different systems. According to one plan, the Government varies

---

[1] This was written before the passing of the Poor Law Amendment Bill. [This is a reference to the Act of 1834 which made the dispensing of poor relief subject to much more stringent provisions than those applied under the Speenhamland system which operated in the southern part of England. As a result of its provisions, expenditure on poor relief was reduced substantially after 1834. Norman himself, as his *Autobiography* relates, was much involved in the administration of the new poor law in Bromley, Kent.

its demands after short intervals, looking to the state of the crops or other peculiar circumstances. The other constitutes what is called the permanent settlement and was introduced by Lord Cornwallis into Bengal. This, though established with the best intentions, seems to have failed on the whole in the expected result of giving security to the cultivators, and encouraging the growth and outlay of capital on the land. The cause of this failure must be sought for, in the circumstance, that the permanent settlement was made not with the ryots or peasants but with the Zemindars who under the native princes collected or farmed the revenue of large districts. The consequence of this mistake has been, that the latter to whom great coercive power was almost necessarily given, have oppressed their dependents, much more than the Government would have done, while owing to their extravagance and bad management, the imaginary advantage of creating a class of wealthy and independent landowners, a turbaned squirearchy has not been attained.

In India, it is said, the land revenue often exceeds the real rent, and falling on profits, ruins the ryots, and prevents the accumulation of capital, and a skilful cultivation of the soil. This is a point which should be carefully attended to. When confined within due limits, the land revenue possesses all the desirable qualities; it is really a burden upon nobody and only prevents the growth of a class of unproductive consumers who are represented by the servants of the state.

In France a heavy tax on rent exists under the name of impôt foncier amounting to above 20 per cent in an average, which is also found, under some other designation in most continental countries. It is difficult for a foreigner to acquire exact details as to the practical operation of these imposts which are usually assessed in conformity to a cadastre, or general survey of all lands. This survey requires the labour of many years, and an immense expenditure of money, and when finished will generally be found inexact and unequal, but if some abuses and defects in the administration should occur, we may be assured, that they are not essential, but would admit of a remedy more or less perfect.

The Taille before the revolution in France, was a tax on rent, of the most partial and oppressive nature, for it only applied to the property of roturiers, persons not noble, it was collected from the occupiers and was administered with the most absurd and cruel harshness and inequality.[2] It was one of the greatest grievances complained of by the Tiers Etat.

---

[2]See Adam Smith Book 5, Chapter 2, Article 2. [Adam Smith *An Inquiry into the Nature and Causes of the Wealth of Nations* (1776) ed. E. Cannan, London: 1904 reprinted London: Methuen, 1961. Part II of Chapter 2 of Smith's book V is almost one hundred pages long (pp. 349-440), being Smith's treatment of taxation. The material on the inequity of the Taille is pp. 381-2.]

Chapter 26

The Poll-Tax

We are now come to an impost of a very complicated nature, as to its effects, but so simple in its details; one which presents itself so obviously to the view of the most unpractised financier, that it has usually been adopted during the infancy of most Nations, and still furnishes a considerable portion of the revenue, in Turkey and Russia, which have not yet reached the level of European civilization. Why it should have been universally abandoned in other countries does not readily appear; objectionable it certainly is in many respects, yet is it preferable to several imposts, which find a place in the revenue of the most enlightened States.

The financial systems of barbarous Nations are ill-arranged; they want neatness and precision and are oppressively collected; but at least they tend directly to their legitimate end, they have no view but that of transferring to the Government a certain portion of the people's wealth, by the shortest and easiest process, they are not founded on absurd theories, which give them a direction diametrically hostile to the best distribution of capital and industry.

The poll-tax if universal falls on every species of property. Persons of all professions are subject to it; in so far as it is paid by the most numerous class, that of Labourers, it usually is indirect. Yet still is noticed here in conformity to the ordinary arrangement.

A general Poll-tax, being paid then by labourers to that extent diminishes profits. It also affects those employing labor unproductively whoever they may be, landowners, annuitants or capitalists. It farther is felt by these classes as consumers, whenever it raises the price of commodities, and also to the extent of their personal assessment.

No data exists to enable us to form an exact estimate of the extent to which the poll-tax as it actually exists possesses many of the desirable qualities, but we may venture to assume that founded on a previous census, it would be moderately computable, simple, constant and non-interferent, except from a tendency, dependent in some degree upon its amount, to foster the adoption of machinery when not naturally required, and also to affect different employments in an unequal degree, uncorruptive and unevasible.

It would be divisible if kept at a moderate amount, but would fail in this respect, if attempted to be raised to an extent, capable of furnishing a large portion of the national expenses, where circumstances require them to be large.

The number of persons called upon to pay it and the small sum demandable, from each might render the collection expensive, but its liability to prodigality would in some degree be corrected by the difficulty of escaping from it and other circumstances.

In general it would be very unpopular, more so indeed than it deserves. This would be the consequence of its being a direct impost, and of its apparent inequality, added to the ignorance prevailing amongst those who paid the largest portion of it, as to the reimbursement they finally received from a rise in wages.

When first established it would be highly unequal, pressing heavily on the labourer who never ought to be exposed to taxation; even after wages had risen, it might still affect him more slightly, from holding out an unnatural inducement to the multiplication of machinery. Like imposts on raw produce, it would fall unequally on capitalists, in comparison with landowners and annuitants. Finally it would be unequal in its effects on the prices of the several commodities calculated to afford either pleasure or utility. One man may require, or may receive pleasure from an article principally produced by machinery; the tax would then diminish his enjoyments in a very trifling degree, or even cheapen them. Another may prefer an article to the production of which a large portion of manual labor is essentially necessary and would be fined for pleasing his taste.

It would be a very vexatious impost, because although the trouble and annoyance of making returns of the number of his household might not be considerable to a given individual, yet the object of the task would render it disagreeable, and it would moreover be imposed, on every head of a family in the Nation: so that the aggregate amount of the grievance, added to the necessary precautions against fraud would be severely felt.

It would be a great improvement on the plan of a poll-tax, if instead of being levied from the laborers themselves, it was assessed on their employers. Suppose the amount to be £2 per head, per annum. The proprietor of a manufactory, employing a 100 workmen, would contribute £200, while the petty tradesman, with two journeymen, would only be called upon for £4. Many difficulties of detail would doubtless present the execution of this plan, but they might readily be surmounted. The only serious objection to this improved poll-tax would be its inequality, and this would spring from four sources, one easily remediable, the other three[1] more difficult of cure. The first would be the situation of landowners and annuitants, under the proposed system which would require to be obviated by a tax on rent, and passive income, the second would be the unnatural tendency to the employment of machinery, instead of men, and the consequent injury to the labouring class, third, the unequal rise in the prices of commodities, and the unequal deduction from the enjoyments of consumers arising from it, fourth, the

---

[1] [Norman had mistakenly written 'two' instead of 'three' at this point.]

different value of the various kinds of labor, which it would probably be necessary to tax alike.

Chapter 27

Legacy Duty and Stamp Duty on Probates of Wills

The legacy duty and stamp duty on probates and letters of administration, are treated of together, because they differ but in name, and offer a specimen of a similar species of absurdity to that exhibited in dividing the tax on the same commodity between the customs and excise, with the effect of increasing trouble and expense to all parties without any corresponding advantage.

These taxes as now existing fall on capitalists and annuitants alone, and afford a curious and instructive example of the effrontery with which a legislature of landowners has ventured to place a heady burden, on the necks of its fellow citizens, while the class to which itself belongs is wholly exempted from them.

These imposts are frugal, non-interferent and unevasible. On the other hand they are incomputable, inconstant and indivisible.

They are also unpopular not so much however from the real grievances which belong to them, as from that dislike which prevails to an absurd and irrational extent in the public mind against all direct taxes whatever, and which also makes them be considered vexatious. That epithet being usually applied in England to any impost in the collection of which it is necessary that the payer should make returns of property, these returns being necessarily subject to examination and revision on the part of the public authorities.

They are highly unequal:

1. As not being levied at all on real property

2. As not being, with the exception of the legacy duty, assessed at the same rate on all property of a similar kind. Reasons have been adduced in the first section, which seem to evince, that it would be inexpedient to make the rich man contribute a larger proportion of his property to the exigencies of the state, than the person of moderate wealth, but that a smaller proportion should be demanded from him as in the present instance, is a revolting piece of injustice. All must allow that a simple equality is the utmost that he can in fairness claim, while many would maintain, that this was too favorable to him.

The following extract from the English scale, will shew how it violates all rules of justice.

	Probate Duty	Letters of Administration
£100 − £200	£2	£3
£100,000 − £120,000	£1500	£2250
£200 − £300	£5	£8
£200,000 − £250,000	£3000	£4500
£300 − £450	£8	£11
£300,000 − £350,000	£4400	£6750

The excess of tax upon letters of administration is justified by no sufficient reasons, they clearly ought to be assimilated.[1]

---

[1] Marshall's Tables, p. 176 – [Marshall op. cit., Part II, p. 176 'Statements shewing the number of *Administrators* to Personal Property, and amount administered to, distinguishing the amount sworn to under Probate, from the amount sworn to under *Letters of Administration*, in the year 1824, and Gross Receipt of the *Legacy*, *Probate*, and all other *Stamp Duties*, in each of the years 1805-1831'. Marshall sets out the scales of duties. Norman's text does not make immediately clear the source of his indignation, but it was due to the taxes on larger estates being proportionately smaller than on small estates, though large in absolute amounts. See J.R. McCulloch *A Treatise on the Principles and Practical Influence of Taxation and the Funding System*, 3rd edition 1863, ed. D.P. O'Brien. Edinburgh: Scottish Academic Press for the Scottish Economic Society, 1975 pp. 295-301.]

That provision which imposes a heavier duty on legatees who are strangers in blood than on relatives, and again on distant than on near relatives seem not to be inconsistent in most cases with the doctrine of equality of sacrifice.

A tax to be uncorruptive should be so arranged, as to give to the payer, both the motive and means to economize its amount, from his expenditure, so as not to diminish his own and the National capital. It has been made a subject to accusation against the property tax, that it does not do this, that it is an impost on capital itself. In that instance, the cause of reproach, if well founded may be readily removed, but in the legacy duty it is less easily remediable. The individual to whom £1,000 is bequeathed, and who receives after deducting the impost we will assume £900, looks at the latter sum alone as the real addition to his fortune, and even if a prudent man does not think it incumbent on him, to carry it to the original, but now nominal amount by an exertion of forbearance. However even here the evil might be removed, if that should be thought requisite, by commuting the demand, now exacted from the executors or administrators previously to the distribution of the assets into an annual charge upon the legatees, proportioned to the value of the property to which they succeed. Security might be taken if required. This change would have the farther effect of rendering the impost more computable, constant, and divisible, than at present; it would however augment its unpopularity, and the expense of collection.

However the great alterations required to cure the inequality, and other evils of the legacy duty &c are:

1. To impose it on all property whatever, including of course land

2. To fix the same proportionate scale on all successions of the same amount, whether bequeathed by will or not, retaining however a discrepancy between strangers and relatives

3. To consolidate the legacy duty and stamps on probates and letters of

administration into one tax.

These changes in addition to that suggested in the last paragraph, would make these taxes as unexceptionable, as any which are to be found in the British scheme of finance, and would render it highly inexpedient to repeal them, except for the purpose of introducing that great and fundamental improvement, which in the present state of the public mind, no ministry could perhaps venture to propose, a commutation of all our National burdens, for one simple impost on income or property.

Chapter 28

The Assessed Taxes and Stamp Duties

The various imposts known by the names of the assessed taxes and stamp duties, have been already examined separately under the several heads to which they respectively belong. It is nevertheless expedient to bestow a little attention upon them, under their collective designations, because the reader will naturally expect to find them thus noticed, and because some observations are required on the qualities which belong to them, as regarded under the legal and popular classification.

The assessed taxes may be divided into those falling on:

1. Objects of luxury, horses, carriages, hair powder, servants &c &c. These are paid by the person using the objects in question. See chapter 19

2. Rent, houses and windows, paid by the owners of houses. See chapter 24

3. Profits, shopmen and commercial clerks.

Some doubt indeed may be entertained whether these last are not really paid for the most part by the consumer, owing to their being partial and extending to comparatively few trades. Under present circumstances they would seem to raise prices in those particular trades. If they were general this consequence would not arise. Buying and selling is merely barter, rendered easy and convenient by the introduction of an universal medium of exchange, and if all commodities are equally taxed, they will stand in the same relation to each other as before, and any tax upon them will merely diminish profits.

The house tax is perhaps the only impost of the whole class which a wise legislature would retain, and that rather as a portion of a general impost on property, than in its present shape.

The inequality of the burden so loudly and justly complained of at present, not by those who really bear it; vizt the owners of shops and small houses in the metropolis, and other large towns, but by the occupiers who are completely exempt from it, except as leaseholders requires, and should receive correction. The difficulty of curing the evil, consists in finding a rule by which to estimate the value of a large mansion, such as Burlington House, compared with one of moderate dimensions, or a shop or other building applied to purposes of trade. The actual or estimated rent of the former, in their present state cannot be considered as a fair basis of taxation. That should be the real amount of property. The extent of protection afforded by the Government, should furnish the measure of the sum to be paid for that protection. The proprietor has no claim for exemption, because he neglects to employ his property to the best advantage.

Thus then in the case of Burlington House, we should take the annual return on the largest sum, which the building itself, and the ground attached to it would fetch in the market, experienced surveyors could readily estimate this, and the result would be an assessment far exceeding that derived from its existing state.

Stamp duties may be divided into those falling on:

1. Justice, law stamps &c &c paid by litigants. See chapter 22.

2. The transfer of property, bill and receipt stamps &c &c paid by buyers

and sellers, chiefly the latter. See chapter 23. Sometimes however they fall on consumers.

3. Knowledge, newspaper stamps, paid by consumers, by those who wish to acquire knowledge. See also chapter 23.

4. Prudence, stamps on insurance policies, paid by those who insure their property, or by consumers. See also chapter 23.

5. Health, stamps on medicines. See again chapter 23.

6. Ingenuity, again chapter 23.

A mere inspection of the above enumeration evinces that the stamp duties, form upon the whole the worst portion of our fiscal system. Hardly one is to be found, which is not a penalty upon, and consequently an obstacle to the performance of some useful, and therefore laudable action; which does not either prevent it altogether, and thus produce unmixed evil, or if the action be performed in spite of it, does not fall with unjust inequality upon him who pays it.

It cannot be denied, but that the stamp duties are convenient, and easy of collection hence their universal adoption. That they are not unpopular with the payers is a lamentable proof of the ignorance which prevails among the public at large, of the circumstances that influence the general welfare. If transferred from useful to pernicious actions, it would be hardly possible to prevent them from giving a sort of public sanction to the latter, by interesting the Government in their continuance, and thus increasing instead of diminishing them, and besides they would yield but little upon this plan, so much does good predominate over evil, in the habits of society, when man is left to his impulses under the protection of enlightened laws. Upon this point the reader is referred to chapter 15, and also to chapter 30.

Chapter 29

Turnpike and Bridge Tolls, Barrières and Harbour and Light Dues

The Turnpike tolls in this country, and the other imposts enumerated in this chapter exactly resemble what the post office charges would be supposing that the sum paid for the conveyance of letters was strictly confined to the cost. On this point the reader is referred to chapter 21.

It is rather remarkable, that Governments among their many ingenious schemes for extracting money from the people, have never attempted to make the former, as well as the latter, a source of revenue.

It is perfectly clear that numerous and good means of communication &c &c are one of the most necessary elements in the progress of wealth and civilization, that the construction and preservation of roads, harbours and light-houses, could never be left wholly to the efforts of individual interest, and that the state must in some shape or other undertake them, making use of the voluntary acts of private persons, to the extent that circumstances may permit.

The English Government discharges this important duty through the means of Turnpikes, duties on shipping, country and parish assessments, and occasionally parliamentary grants. The first only need be examined here, as the representative of the whole class to which it belongs. What is said of toll-bars as a mode of levying the money requisite for the making and maintenance of roads will be readily applied by the reader, to the other objects enumerated at the head of this chapter.

Considered as a tax, Turnpike tolls fall generally on the first payer, who however is reimbursed in case they are paid with a commercial object, by the extra price he is enabled to charge for his commodities or services.

They are always simple, but are popular, non-interferent and uncorruptive in consequence only of their object and small amount, for their tendency is the reverse, and if raised so as to furnish a source of revenue for general purposes, they would be highly objectionable under these heads; thus resembling the post office revenue. But the strongest objection that can be urged against them, is the heavy expense of collection. There is:

1. The allowance to collectors and their perquisites

2. The erection and repair of houses and gates

It is impossible to calculate the amount of these two last items but they must be very considerable. In rural districts many gates may be found yielding less than £150 per annum, where the charges in salary, interest, and repair cannot be less than £50 or above 30 per cent.

The loss of time to the payer, which though apparently small to each individual is still large in the aggregate, especially when compared with the sum raised and may be considered as making them vexatious.

Turnpike tolls appear to be unequal, and are so to a certain extent. It is clear that everybody is interested in their object, the maintenance of good roads &c and the degree of interest may be fairly measured by the amount of property which each person possesses. That should then be the scale of payment. Now a portion of the Turnpike tolls falls on the consumers of certain commodities and services, whose prices have been raised by them, and the remainder on travellers, and it is very possible that an individual may escape his fair share of the burden in both ways, while he derives his full allotment of advantage from the greater efficiency which easy communications afford to the operations of capital, and from the general advance of wealth consequent upon them. The class of laborers who, when travelling by a stage, pay as heavily for tolls as their wealthy neighbours have here especial grounds of complaint.

The permission to carry manure toll-free is a source of inequality in England; another instance of the influence of the landed interest in the legislature, and it should be suppressed, its only effect being to raise rents. The exemption from toll to persons going to a place of worship on Sunday is also unequal, but there the object in view may scarcely excuse the anomaly. It may be said moreover, that it is the interest of all, that as many as possible should be attracted to the performance of this important religious duty.

It now only remains to say a few words on the question:

Is it advisable to retain the system of tolls in England, or to provide for the roads &c from the general revenues of the State as is done in France?

Arguing from general principles alone, we should perhaps say, that the latter plan was the best, that the greatest degree of frugality, non-interference and equality might be attained by it, but looking to experience as a guide, judgment must be given the other way. By Turnpikes the money is collected in driblets, the payers hardly feel it; it never passes either into or out of the hands of the central Government, and neither the legislature, or people are fully cognizant of its amount. Was it to figure annually in the ministerial budget, it is to be feared, that both would unite in diminishing too much the expenditure on an object of the greatest public utility, which does not dazzle the eye in the shape of uniform or ermine.

In Great Britain the roads are said to cost near four millions a year, and it maybe doubted whether Parliament would consent to devote half as much to such a purpose; 8 millions or 200 millions of francs is named as the sum requisite to put in order the broad, strait sloughs, which by courtesy are called roads in France.

It must also be allowed that usually, though not universally, the amount that can be readily raised by tolls, forms a measure of the sum that ought to be expanded on a particular line of road, and thus sometimes furnishes an useful check to extravagance. On the whole it seems clear that if some well founded objections may be made, against this mode of levying money, it is still preferable to the great mass of taxation which under the supposition of throwing the expense on the National Treasury would supply its place.

Whether the administration of the roads should belong to the central Government, or the districts, is a matter of important consideration but would carry us too far. It may be observed however that the result of a careful analysis would probably be, to leave the high roads to the former, and the cross roads to the latter.

Chapter 30

Taxes on Vices

The title of this chapter would seem to promise a class of imposts to which no friend of humanity could object, which should at once diminish crime and serve to fill the exchequer. The sequel will shew that these apparent advantages are by no means realized. The reader is referred to chapter 15 for some observations which would otherwise find a place here.

Taxes on gaming houses fall wholly on their frequenters. The sum derived by the Government from lotteries, on the foolish and ignorant purchasers of tickets.

The first species of tax never existed in this country, the latter has happily been abolished. This circumstance renders it impossible to investigate all their effects, with the same precision as may be attained with respect to those now in operation.

The lottery yielded to the revenue in 1825 £295,000, the salaries to the commissioner and other expenses were £13,000 to this is to be added advertising and the various means which are used to propagate delusion, and which are said to have cost here above £30,000 annually.[1] Then come the

---

[1] See Marshall – Sheet and p. 194. [See Marshall, op. cit.; the reference by Norman is to one of the folding sheets at the beginning of Part II of Marshall, op. cit. It is 'Statement No. III – Of the Annual Income and Expenditure of the Government of Great Britain' and covers the years 1793-1832. Line 13 'Lottery' shows revenue for 1825 of £295,390. Expenses are shown on p. 194 of Marshall as £13,000. State lotteries were abolished by the Lotteries Act, 1823. This did not however take effect immediately; 1825 seems to

other disbursements of the contractor if the impost be farmed, the allowance to their agents, and finally their profits. All these several items are paid by the purchasers of tickets and form strictly a part of the expense of collection.

Both these imposts are incomputable, inconstant, indivisible, unequal. On the other hand they are simple and popular, slightly if at all interferent, and unvexatious.

The prodigality of lotteries has been already dilated on. The tax on gaming houses is frugal. Both are evasible, the latter most so.

Up to this point, these taxes, though open to many objections, are certainly not inferior, perhaps preferable to many which contribute to fill the English exchequer. There is only one more point of view, under which they require examination, are they corruptive? Do they tend to foster immorality? Do they act as penalties on indulgence of hurtful propensities, or do they open the gates and smooth the road which leads to ruin and despair? The answer is obvious. The licence to gaming houses gives a public sanction to them, and invests them with a certain kind of respectability, their frequenters feel a sort of security against the grosser tricks of an infamous traffic which specially allures the inexperienced. Gaming is most common and destructive when the houses in which it is carried on pay a contribution to, and are consequently protected by the Government.

Lotteries when not made to yield a revenue are almost always forbidden Their ill-effects are distinctly perceived when the legislature is unwilling or unable from the influence of public opinion to raise an income from them. The same thing is true of[2] gaming houses, they are prohibited when untaxed. Their number, or at any rate the resort to them is diminished, they are held to be infamous, the popular sanction is turned against them. In other words when there is no tax there is least gaming. Surely these considerations decide

---

have been the last full year of operation, though a revenue of £100,000 was reported by Marshall for 1826.]

[2][Norman has 'from' in the manuscript.]

the question of corruptiveness.

The only grounds upon which these taxes can be defended, is the affirmation that no evil arises from the countenance and protection given, because a certain portion of the passion for play must exist, and no harm can therefore arise from the raising a revenue from its gratification. But it has been sufficiently shown, that the passion is excited where it would not otherwise exist, or at least intensified, by the means adopted to enrich the exchequer.

Whether a wise Government ought so far to interfere with the free agency of the people as to prohibit every species of gaming, or to what extent it should be allowed is a question which does not belong to the present essay, but this may be affirmed with the utmost confidence, that no prudent legislature would encourage practices, productive of acute and extended misery.

Chapter 31

The Income Tax in England

Having now surveyed the most important of the various partial imposts which have existed in this country, it remains only to examine the income tax the most general and in some respects the best source of revenue, that the skill of our financiers has ever yet devised, but which nevertheless was snatched from their grasp in the year 1816 by the legislature with the approbation of the whole Nation, as the readiest means of checking ministerial extravagance. This item in our fiscal catalogue has been reserved till now because what has been previously said, as is usual in an ascent from particulars to generals, will tend to shorten and facilitate the enquiry into its nature and effects.

The income tax was designed to place at the disposal of the Government ten per cent of the income of every individual possessing wealth in the community, whether this income was derived from land, from money placed at interest, from trade, or from professional services, with some relaxation in favor of those at the bottom of the scale. It thus fell upon landowners, annuitants and capitalists. It was in theory a tax on rent and profits of ten per cent, with the curious exception that $7\frac{1}{2}$ per cent on the rental paid by the occupiers was the amount of contribution imposed on them. In the case of private leasehold houses it may be assumed that this portion of the impost usually fell upon the proprietors, but it may be here asked, why should not the $7\frac{1}{2}$ per cent paid by farmers fall on landowners, as that paid by house occupiers did on house owners? Because the first are always capitalists, the latter not so. The mass of profits being taxed those of farmers could not escape from the common burthen; the effects of competition obliged them to submit to their share of it. Had they refused and insisted on a proportionate reduction of rent, other capitalists would have stepped forwards and offered to pay the tax. Houses or buildings let for trading purposes resemble farms in this respect

At the point of equality among themselves, the whole body of capitalists would not have had the power of throwing the load on other classes. We must here however remark that taxation cannot permanently reduce profits below a certain level. Still lower in the scale, capitals will emigrate and be spent unproductively, or wasted in abortive speculations.

The income tax without being thoroughly computable, divisible and certain owing to the errors in its machinery, was more so, than any other tax, and in point of simplicity, was equally distinguished, reference being had to the large amount derived from it.

It was probably very frugal.

In the year 1815 the gross produce was £16,548,000, the net produce £15,298,000 and the expense of collection and all deductions therefore about eight per cent, the greater portion of the difference belonged to the second head.[1]

No distinct account of the simple expense of collection has been discovered.

---

[1] [Marshall p. 27 gives figures of £16,548,986 gross and £15,298,983 net. The biggest share of this (more than one third) was that contributed by Schedule A, levied on the proprietors of land. It was thus a property tax. The details of the assessments by county for England and Wales, with a single figure for Scotland, are in Marshall p. 30. See J. Marshall *A Digest of All the Accounts Relating to the Population, Productions, Revenues, Financial Operations, Manufactures, Shipping, Colonies, Commerce, &c. &c. of the United Kingdom of Great Britain and Ireland. Part II. A Statistical Display of the Finances, Navigation and Commerce of the United Kingdom of Great Britain and Ireland.* London: printed by J. Haddon by Recommendation of the Select Committee of the House of Commons on Public Documents, 1833.]

The unpopularity of the tax was excessive and finally occasioned its abolition. This might be ascribed in some respects to the real evils belonging to it, of which the greater and more important part however admitted of easy removal or alleviation, but was owing chiefly to that extreme dislike of direct taxes, which seems so characteristic of the English people. It was thoroughly non-interferent.

The best founded objection to it arose from its inequality.

Taxation to be equal should abstract from each individual an equal proportion of his wealth, thus a landowner with an income of £4,000 arising from an estate worth £100,000 should pay £1,000, while a merchant with an equal income, arising from a capital of £40,000 paid only £400, and a physician with the same income perhaps not more than £200, as his, revenue would depend on the continuance of life, health, and popular favor, and could hardly therefore be considered to represent a capital of more than £20,000 or in other words to be worth more than 5 years purchase; according to the scheme of the English income tax these several persons all contribute alike.

It has been proved in the chapter 12 that the proper basis of an equal taxation is property. If instead of adopting this basis directly, that of income be preferred, the end in view may be attained by fixing a different rate of contribution on the various classes of society, possessing the same amount of income according to the principal, which their annual revenue may be supposed to represent.

This rule being kept in view, the following short table will exhibit striking proof of the utter violation of justice which ensued from the impost now under consideration.

Table showing the amount paid to the income tax by persons each possessing £1,000 per annum, and what they ought to have paid under an equal system of taxation, at the rate of $\frac{2}{5}$ths per cent on property.

The favor shewn to the landed interest, which has been so often before remarked cannot here escape observation. A similar tendency may also be

	Income	Principal	Tax	Equal Proportion
Landowner	£1000	£25,000	£100	£100
Freeholder – In 3 per				
cent the price at 60	£1000	£20,000	£100	£80
Merchant	£1000	£10,000	£100	£40
Physician or Placeman	£1000	£5000	£100	£20

suspected in the provision which made the occupier of a farm liable to a payment of $7\frac{1}{2}$ per cent on the rent as a sort of composition for the tax the result was a scale of contribution inferior to that imposed on the productive classes in general, and at any rate unequal as respected the individuals subject to it, as is clear when we compare the capitals employed by a grazier, and by the tenant on a heavy tillage farm. But perhaps this anomaly is to be ascribed less to the sinister interest of the legislature, than to the facility of assessment derived from it.

The circumstance that the income tax was levied purely on revenue introduced occasionally a new and peculiar species of inequality. It was levied from insolvent traders and thus became a tax upon their creditors. Instances have existed whereby in consequence of large profits having accrued in the very year when a commission of bankruptcy was issued against a mercantile firm, the sum thus unjustly levied has been very considerable.

It must be allowed that the theoretic inequality of the income tax was balanced in a great degree by the superior means of escape from it possessed by the various mercantile and professional classes of which they largely availed themselves.

The entire immunity or at least the great favor allowed to persons of very small fortune, may be considered by some as a ground of inequality. Upon this point the reader is referred to chapter 12.

The income tax was perfectly uncorruptive as far as regarded, landowners, freeholders, mortgagees and in fact every class of persons, except those employed in trade and professions. For the former there was no escape, no means of evasion, and consequently no allurement to roguery. The same thing cannot be said of the latter. The slight scrutiny to which these were exposed held out inducements to perjury against which the integrity of many strove in vain. So far all will perhaps agree, but most will say that the examination to which the books and transactions of persons engaged in business were necessarily subjected was in itself a great evil, that it was injurious and productive of bad consequences by unfolding the true situation of mercantile men in other words that it was corruptive. This view of the subject involved the assumption that the community derives advantages from the ignorance prevailing as to the fortunes of traders; surely the very reverse is demonstrably true. Were all to know the real situation of every man in business, the evils of insolvency would almost disappear. Even taking the most favorable case, that of A, who we will suppose to possess nothing, though imagined to be worth £20,000, the false credit which he has acquired may enable him to protract the period of bankruptcy, and to occasion by abortive efforts to restore his affairs, increased loss to his creditors. But even he would gain in an equal degree by knowing the precise situation of B.C.D. and the rest of the alphabet. It may indeed now and then happen, that A being at one period insolvent, under the protection of secrecy, may right himself by a successful speculation, but experience shews that this case is excessively rare. The public feeling on this point seems only fit for the Fleet or the King's Bench. The best means of enforcing such a degree of enquiry into the situation of traders as might be necessary in order to levy the tax, is a point which will be considered hereafter. The income tax was very vexatious, its inquisitorial nature, and the large amount which it required to be paid directly into the hands of the tax-gatherer, revolted popular opinion, and were the great causes of its removal.

It was almost perfectly unevasible, excepting with respect to professional persons and traders. These possessed ready means of escaping from its grasp, and used them without scruple.

Chapter 32

An Improved Property Tax

The subject of the present chapter is so wide and complicated, that to examine it in all its details, would occupy alone an extensive work; this then will not be attempted. All that can be done is to sketch the plan of one great impost intended to supersede the heterogenous mass of taxes, which now furnish the revenue of this and other countries, filling up the framework to such an extent only as may be required in order to shew the superiority which this scheme of finance would possess over that now in operation. The reader is referred to chapters 4, 12 and 31, for many observations bearing on the matter now in hand, and which it is unnecessary to repeat.

Hereafter the author, should his views be favorably received by the public, may endeavour to complete the picture: but even should he fail in the attempt, should he not succeed in wholly removing all difficulties and silencing every objection, it will not follow that his general principles are incorrect or that his scheme itself is impracticable. The financial systems of Nations, as they now exist, are the result of the labours of Government for many ages. The most acute and ingenious men have been employed upon them, and it may be supposed that in many respects they have received all the ameliorations of which they are susceptible. Even if a very small proportion of the same toil and talent should be devoted without success to remove the obstacles and inconvenience attendant on his system, it might be allowed to be a failure.

This system consists in the abolition of all the taxes now in operation, and their replacement by one general impost on property, which should take from each person possessing wealth in the community, an equal proportion of that wealth. The propriety of adopting the same scale of contribution from all fortunes whether large or small, has already been defended at length. This would not however prevent some relaxation towards those at the bottom of the ladder, should it be deemed expedient as a matter of convenience. Even should a scale of contribution increasing with the increase of individual wealth, be thought more consistent, with the true doctrine of equality of sacrifice; no change would be necessary in any thing but the scale itself. The arguments in favor of the general plan would remain untouched.

The tax on property here proposed, should be levied according to a general assessment corrected every year, and placed under the eye of the legislature at the commencement of every session. The sum to be demanded from each contributor should be that resulting from the amount of his property in the year preceding; and in order that no accidental misfortune to individuals accruing subsequently to the completion of the annual registration might occasion loss or inconvenience to the Government, the whole territory should be divided into districts, whose inhabitants should be collectively responsible. This provision could hardly add much to the burdens of individuals while it would materially diminish the danger arising from private dishonesty as each man would have a direct interest in discovering and checking the frauds of his neighbours.

In order to afford the best opportunity for public criticism, a list of the persons taxed, with their residences the amount of their property and the sum demandable from each, should be affixed in some public place for general inspection.

The incomes of annuitants should be capitalised according to fixed rules, under which the age, sex and profession &c of the parties should be distinguished and allowed for.

The fiscal districts might be formed, of parishes, hundreds, and counties. So that the first should be liable, with certain limitations perhaps, for the defalcation of its inhabitants, the second for the defalcations in the first, and the third for those in the second. Or it would be better in consequence of the irregularities in point of size and of the existing territorial division, to make a new demarcation. In this it would be desirable to blend together towns and rural districts, in order to afford as much compensation as possible in the event of partial misfortunes. The tax when it fell on real property directly, or on a mortgage or other charge on real property, should be paid where the property was situated, and not where the owner might reside. This at any rate should be the general rule, though another arrangement might perhaps occasionally be allowed to suit private convenience.

One essential piece of machinery for the carrying into effect this plan, would be a general system of registration, of a more extensive nature, than any hitherto employed, which should extend to all property whatever subjected to the tax. It would comprehend not merely what is found in the registers of our colonies, of Ireland, Scotland and continental countries, but also the capitals of commercial men, the gains of lawyers, physicians &c, the salaries of employers whether public or private, and the incomes of annuitants. The revenues of all the last named classes would require to be capitalized.

Let not the imagination of the reader be terrified with the picture here portrayed to him. Let him not think that the proposed scheme is an unattainable chimera. In order to shew how unfounded would be such an apprehension it is only necessary to point out how much of its exists already in this or other countries, and what will be wanting to complete it.

Thus bonds of all sorts are registered in Denmark, and Norway. Annuities in England, and in France a trader is obliged to keep a journal and to make out a balance sheet once a year, and it is ordained that these docu-

ments 'seront cotés, paraphés, et visés soit par un des juges des Tribunauxe
de Commerce, soit par le Maire ou un adjoint dans la forme ordinaire et
sans fraix'.[1] Without this formality they cannot be produced as evidence,
in Courts of Justice, in favor of those to whom they belong. Though this
provision of the French law is not employed for fiscal purposes, yet it is important as shewing that the distinguished jurists, who framed the existing
code, did not imagine that a balance of good was likely to be produced by
throwing an impenetrable veil over the operations of merchants and in as
much as this law, promulgated the 20th September 1807 was unrepealed in
1827 and probably still continues in force it is clear that experience had not
revealed any inconveniences which rendered its abolition necessary.

In Norway a tax exists called Byskat or Town Tax, which it is intended
should be levied in proportion to the wealth and income of each individual. It
is assessed by a commission chosen by the taxpayers from the town or district
who are supposed to be well-acquainted with the pecuniary circumstances of
their neighbours, and who thus form a sort of jury.

Mr Urquahrt in his work on Turkey[2] makes many sensible observations
on the plan of direct contributions which now exists there, and points out

---

[1] See Art 11, Tit. 2 of the Code de Commerce. ['Les livres dont la tenue est ordonné
par les art. 8 et 9 ci-dessus seront cotés, paraphés et visés soit par un des juges des
tribunaux de commerce, soit par le maire ou un adjoint dans la forme ordinaire et sans
frais. Les commerçants seront tenus de conserver ces livres pendant dix ans.' (The books
of which the keeping is required by articles 7 and 8 above shall be completed, initialled, and
countersigned either by one of the judges of the commercial tribunal or by the mayor or a
deputy mayor in the ordinary method of procedure and without charge. The tradespeople
are bound to keep these books for ten years.) See *Les Codes Annotés de Sirey*, ed. P.
Gilbert, Paris: Marchal et Cie, 1865, Vol. II, p. 12, *Code de Commerce Titre II. Des Livres
de Commerce art. 11*. Article 8 laid down detailed requirements including a day-book,
with accounts receivable and payable, commercial operations, negotiations, acceptances
and endorsements, and in general all payments into and out of the business under any
head, and, month by month, the sums employed in the business, and all of this independent
of the other books necessarily employed by the business. In addition firms were required
to keep together letters received, and copies of letters sent. It is remarkable that Norman,
a man of business until his early retirement in 1830, at the age of 37, should have been
willing to advocate such a degree of commercial supervision. Whether this passage was
written before or after his retirement is not known.]

[2] [D. Urquhart *Turkey and Its Resources*. London: Saunders and Otley, 1833.]

the beneficial effects consequent upon it when properly administered. The mode of assessment by an elected jury might furnish the means of sparing the feelings of those, in whose minds the existing prejudice as to the advantages derived from enveloping in secrecy the transactions of traders, should continue to hold their ground. This Jury should consist of neighbours whose verdict might be appealed against either by the taxpayer or an officer of the Government and the final decision be left to a higher tribunal. It is unnecessary here to point out how such a tribunal should be formed.

The whole tax should be divided into two or more portions, and the payment be fixed at determinate periods, so contrived as to render the disbursement as little onerous as possible.

In the last chapter, and in chapters 4, 12 and 13, it has been sufficiently shewn that a due enquiry into the circumstances of traders considered by itself, and without any fiscal views, would be a great good. Some important effects heretofore unnoticed may be now pointed out; increased caution on the part of merchants, a better and more careful mode of keeping accounts, an improved morality with respect to pecuniary liabilities. It is unnecessary to insist upon the advantages which would flow from the virtuous and useful impulses thus given, or on the mischief arising from the want of them.

In this country, a strong line of distinction wholly unwarranted by reason, is drawn between farmers and other traders. This should be abolished. He who cultivates the soil is as much a person engaged in commerce, as he who keeps a grocer's shop, or a silk factory; all should be ruled by the same laws.

From what has been said it is clear that the regulations now demanded for the purpose of establishing a perfect system of taxation already exist, or have existed in this or other countries to a considerable extent, with more or less completeness. The point on which the greatest deficiency is to be found is the incomes of professional men. The advantages per se arising from the obligations laid upon merchants to keep and exhibit proper accounts, does not apply with equal weight to them. Still it cannot be proved that any real injury beyond a little trouble, would be inflicted on them by the enforcements of such a practice, and if so, the general good, ought to overbalance any partial inconvenience.

It must however again be remarked, that no practical injustice would be committed, if such persons were to be exempted altogether from the tax. Their incomes may be considered chiefly as a return for the expenses of their education &c &c, and will thus be affected in the long run by whatever influences the average rate of profits. If taxation diminishes the profits of traders, it will also from the effects of competition diminish the income of the class now spoken of. There can be no doubt but that professional fees would fall ultimately, if all the indirect imposts, which now raise the prices of commodities, the objects of expenditure, were to be removed. The importance of this observation must excuse its repetition.

The best mode of taxing placemen is to lower their salaries.

The commutation of existing burdens into one general tax on property would wholly cure the most important of the evils, flowing from the National Debt, vizt, the maintenance of impolitic taxes employed to pay the interest and would besides render its redemption in whole or part should that be deemed expedient, a comparatively easy operation.

As it is not at present the author's aim to construct a detailed plan for a general property tax, but merely to offer a slight sketch calculated to evince, that such an impost does not involve in its nature any practical obstacles which can be considered invincible, it only remains to examine how far it would possess the desirable qualities. After all that has been said this enquiry need be but short.

A property tax as above described, would be computable in the highest possible degree, because the general wealth, and its division among the whole mass of citizens would be known in each year before the proportion of contribution was fixed, as well as the amount demandable from each person.

It would be far more simple than the ill-assorted congeries of imposts that now fills the exchequer, and would cost in collection after the necessary machinery had been once established, a small proportion only of what is now thus expended.

It would constitute the only financial system that can even be conceived, which would be perfectly constant and divisible, which could be thoroughly depended on, as a means of defraying the charges of Government, except under the highly improbable circumstance, of a sudden diminution in the national wealth or a disturbance in the machinery of society, and such convulsions, would still more disorganize any other fiscal arrangement.

In the present state of the public mind however, a general property tax, would be highly unpopular, so much so as to render its imposition with a view to supply the whole revenue, practically impossible. If however the arguments which have been adduced in its favor are convincing, it follows that the dislike to it, is founded in ignorance and prejudice and may be expected to give place to a directly opposite sentiment, when sounder views and more accurate information shall generally prevail. On this point the author would venture to appeal to posterity against the sentence of his own generation.

A general property tax would be absolutely and entirely non-interferent. Every-body would be left to employ his capital or labor as he might judge to be most for his own interest exactly as if no tax at all existed. Few can even picture to themselves, how greatly such a state of things would aid the progress of wealth, and augment the general mass of enjoyment. It is the only tax which admits of being made thoroughly equal, whether that equality should be sought for in a similar proportionate contribution, as upon the whole the author is inclined to believe, or in a scale rising with the wealth of individuals.

It would be far less corruptive than the present system, none could gain by evading it but those finally called upon to pay it, and none could hope to escape from it but persons employed in trade and professions. The integrity of the rest of the community would be therefore unassailed. The necessary examination into the wealth of persons, belonging to these two classes has been shewn not to be in itself an evil. Even should weight attach to the objection of Mr Ricardo, in consequence of this tax holding out no invitation to the payer to economize its amount, an objection which does not seem important,[3] the impost might be changed into an income tax, varying with the kind of property from which it was derived. This however would injure the unity and completeness of the scheme, and be otherwise inconvenient. Under present circumstances it would be thought highly vexatious by a large portion of the community, its unpopularity indeed would be founded chiefly on this circumstance, and to a certain extent is perhaps excuseable.

Some persons will always be found, who wish to be thought richer or poorer than they are, and by whom publicity along with the means used for attaining it, will be considered an intolerable evil.

It would be thoroughly inevasible, except on the part of the mercantile and professional classes, though even as respects them, it would not be difficult to remove a large portion of the mischief.

---

[3] [It is not clear where Norman obtained this view of Ricardo's opinion. In the *Principles* (op. cit., p. 153) Ricardo criticises the legacy duty as falling on capital because legatees had no incentive to reduce consumption to maintain capital, and thus paid legacy duty out of the proceeds of an inheritance. He does not advance the argument which Norman attributes to him here. In a speech of 16 May 1822, he raised the possibility that a property tax could lead to capital flight, and in a letter to his friend Trower of 9 March 1816 he had expressed the view that a property tax could encourage government extravagance, a view with which McCulloch agreed (letter to Ricardo of 15 May 1820). See *The Works and Correspondence of David Ricardo* ed. P. Sraffa, Cambridge 1951-5, Vol. V, p. 187; Vol. VII, p. 27; Vol. VIII, p. 190. But nowhere does he seem to have expressed the view attributed to him by Norman. However Norman, as a founder member of the famed Political Economy Club, was personally familiar with Ricardo, and had taken part with him in discussions on tax issues. On 4 February 1822, 4 March 1822, and 1 April 1822, Norman had proposed to a meeting of the Club the following question 'What would be the best mode of Taxation?'. At all three meetings Ricardo was present. See H. Higgs (ed.) *Political Economy Club 1821-1920*, Centenary Volume, London: Macmillan, 1921, pp.1, 10-14. As Norman records in his *Autobiography*, he had started his *Essay on Taxation* late the previous year. He also refers to his participation in Political Economy Club meetings, and his admiration for Ricardo.]

Chapter 33

Proposals for Reform

The complete change in our financial system, consequent upon the adoption of the plan sketched in the last chapter, however desirable in itself, however well-calculated to minimize the necessary evils of taxation could never be adopted in the present state of the public mind. Its unpopularity would be so great as to overthrow any efforts which an enlightened Government might make for its establishment. The people as yet are almost completely ignorant upon the subject and in this, as in other instances if we are unable to do, all the good we would, we must be content to do all the good we can. In the meantime the benevolent ought not to be discouraged at the painful spectacles occasionally presented to their gaze, such as the resistance to the house tax one of the least pernicious of our imposts, which only produced about £130,000 and that on the part of a class of persons who did not really pay it,[1] while the corn laws, the excise, and stamp duties, which burden the Nation in a forty-fold degree, hardly excite any opposition. On the contrary, such an example of ignorance and prejudice, should only stimulate the good and wise to fresh efforts, and induce them to exert themselves, each in his particular sphere to dissipate the gloom that surrounds him, and spread abroad the blessed light of reason and of truth. Sooner or later sounder views on the subject of taxation, than now exist will infallibly prevail; in the

---

[1][See note p. 189 on the produce of the house tax.]

meantime the Government should endeavour to palliate difficulties which it cannot overcome, and the object of the present chapter is to point out how they may be effected.

The best mode of treating the matter in hand seems to be:

1. To consider how far economy in the expenditure may be pushed

2. To add to such taxes now in operation, as are most consonant with sound principles and to extract through their means the largest sum which they are capable of yielding

3. To devise new sources of revenue which may be less pernicious than those now existing

4. To apply the resources thus provided in lieu of the worst of our present imposts which should consequently be abolished

A few observations will be made upon each of the above heads, but it must be remarked that a plan well-digested and matured in all its points will not even be aimed at; useful hints can alone be expected in a matter foreign to the general scope of this work, which would require a great space and much labor for its complete elucidation.

1. As to reduction in the National Expenditure, it cannot be safely assumed, that more than two millions per annum may be saved from the present expenses of the State, and even such a saving would be dependent upon the continuance of internal, and external tranquility. Confusion at home or war abroad would vastly augment the demands on the Exchequer, and a political revolution would swell them to an enormous degree as it almost invariably has done in other countries.

   Should the public mind become enlightened on the subject of our foreign dominions, could the people be persuaded, that distant possessions are almost always a burden and ought usually to be gotten rid of, unless they can be made to pay their expenses, except when the national faith is pledged in an opposite direction, we might look for a greater reduction; but of this general advance in political knowledge, there seems at present little chance, and we cannot venture to speculate upon it.

2. As to the addition to or modification of existing taxes.

The first that presents itself is the Legacy Duty. This extended to real, as well as personal property, should be consolidated with the stamp duty on probates. It should also be carried to the same rate in all parts of the scale; at present less is paid in proportion on large than on small fortunes. The amount produced by these taxes in 1831 was £2,021,398, and the result of the proposed changes would probably be to double the produce.[2] In order to meet the well-founded objection to the corruptiveness of the impost as falling on capital, instead of income, provision should be made to enable the payers to discharge the claim by installments, instead of at once, if they choose so to do, interest being added to each. In order that the annual receipt at first might not be too much diminished by this arrangement, encouragement might be held out to private lenders,[3] to advance the amount of the tax on the security of the estates on which it was levied. In most cases this would be done by a private bargain between the parties without any interference on the part of the Government, and a few years practice would create a machinery for the purpose which would work with great facility. Companies, and private capitalists would look in this direction for a regular employment of their funds, and on the whole it seems clear, that an increase to the revenue of two million annually might be expected from the new tax.

---

[2]See Marshall's Tables p.17. [Marshall op. cit. p. 17 gives the produce of the legacy duty for 1831 as £1,144,459 and of the probate duty as £876,239, making a total of £2,021,398.]

[3][The manuscript has 'leaders'.]

It may be urged as an objection to this plan, that testamentary dispositions have been made, and expectations formed, upon the faith of the continuance of the present partiality to the landed interests. But to this it may be answered that no man has a right to complain, if he is only called upon to pay in the same proportion as his neighbour for the advantages of Government, still less can he demand that these advantages should be furnished to him gratis, with respect to one heavy burden. The converse of these propositions would perpetuate in-equality, and indeed every species of existing abuse.

It is unnecessary to enquire whether or not any change is desirable in the proportion paid respectively by persons standing in the different degrees of relationship to, or unconnected in blood with, the deceased. On a cursory view the existing scale does not appear quite consistent with the doctrine of equality; but public opinion sanctions it, and in this instance perhaps equality of sacrifice, and equality of payment do not exactly coincide.

The strong desire which most people possess to retain the command over their property as long as they can, would probably be a sufficient obstacle to the substitution of gifts during life time, in lieu of testamentary bequests, as a means of eluding the impost, but should such a practice become much more common than at present, it would be necessary and perhaps not difficult to devise a legislative remedy for the evil.

The inequality of the existing Land Tax suggests the notion of augmenting it upon the property now assessed at much below the average amount, but perhaps the National faith is pledged to the present arrangement and we must not look for any resource in this quarter.

The house tax should be restored, and carried to an amount equal to what it formerly produced, added to what is now yielded by the window tax which should consequently be abolished. The mode of assessment should be modified accordingly to the plan proposed in chapter 27 – and at the expiration of existing leases the owner and not the occupier should be directly subject to the burden. The increases to the revenue from the proposed alteration would amount to from £1,000,000 to £1,200,000, as the house tax in 1831 yielded £1,178,000.[4]

The so justly reprobated system of timber duties which now cost the country more than a million per annum besides the sum they yield to the exchequer, afford the next item of possible and prudent augmentation. They should be abolished, and replaced by a duty of 30s per load of 50 cubic feet on all timber whatever, no distinction being made between European and Colonial as the total quantity of timber imported amounts to from 900,000 to 1,000,000 loads, and would of course increase after a large reduction in the duty. The impost now proposed would certainly yield £1,500,000 per annum, consequently an increase of about £300,000, upon the sum received from the timber duties in 1831 which was about £1,200,000,[5] while the country would

---

[4]See Marshall's Tables p. 21. [See Marshall, op. cit., Part II, p. 21. Marshall however gives £1,178,470 as the produce of the *window* tax rather than of the house tax. The latter is reported to have yielded £1,357,207. House taxes were introduced in 1696, and abolished in 1834, but re-introduced in 1851. The window tax, also introduced in 1696, was abolished in 1851. Marshall, op. cit., p. 20 provides some information on the house and window taxes which sheds light on the nature of Norman's complaint. In 1821 the total of inhabited houses in Great Britain was 2,429,730 of which 492,186 were charged with duty assessed at £1,264,754. 214,239 farm houses occupied by tenants were exempted. In 1825, 171,739 other houses were exempted, on the grounds of having a rental of less than £10. The number of houses subject to window duty in 1821 was 968,008 and the assessment was £2,578,570. 681,496 cottages were exempt. In 1823 half the window duty was repealed and, in 1825, 634,936 of the 968,008 houses assessed in 1821, but not having more than seven windows, were exempted. McCulloch was scathing about the exemptions from the tax which, he believed, was capable of yielding, at 10 per cent, a revenue of £2.8 million. See the first edition of his *Treatise on the Principles and Practical Influence of Taxation and the Funding System*, London: Longman 1845 pp. 70-73.]

[5]See Marshall's Tables p. 7. [See Marshall, op. cit.. Part II, p. 7. Marshall gives the figures for the produce of the various timber duties under ten different heads, from 1814 to 1831. The total for 1831 was £1,189,379. However ibid. p. 203 shows the timber imports to have fluctuated widely in amount after the ending of the war in 1815. Imports (recorded as loads of 50 cubic feet) for 1815 were 316,716 (Baltic 194,504), for 1820 they were 373,655 (Baltic 65,842), for 1825 they were 754,497 (Baltic 286,871), and for 1831 they were 533,071 (Baltic 146,202). The timber duties were complex, and a major problem for Norman during his years of running the family timber importing business. For long the tax on timber imported from Britain's North American possessions was ten shillings per load, and that on timber from Northern Europe, the 'Baltic' trade (and Norman imported from Norway) was 55s per load. See McCulloch, op. cit., pp. 219-20.]

gain at least £700,000 per annum in the price and quality of the article consumed even after a larger sum in duty than is now paid had been levied upon it.

An ad-valorem duty would in this, as in other instances be less interferent than one by measurement as now proposed, but would hardly be found practicable.

It is doubtless inexpedient upon general principles to burden such an article as timber with an impost amounting probably to 30 or 40 per cent on the selling price, especially considering its tendency to raise in a somewhat similar proportion the price of all timber produced at home, but the proposed plan would at any rate be a great improvement on the existing system, and afford material advantages to the consumer, and among conflicting difficulties we must choose the least.

The next point to be examined is, whether or not we can devise any new taxes less pernicious than those now in operation, to which the Nation might be induced to submit.

The first that naturally suggests itself is a very light property tax. This has been pointed out as the only efficient resource, by almost every writer on the subject of financial reform; the most distinguished statesmen have expressed their approbation of it, and have deplored the impossibility of having recourse to it, owing to the repugnance of the public to direct taxation. This repugnance might be diminished:

1. By making the establishment of the impost coincide with the abrogation of many others, and to a larger amount

2. By fixing it [at] a very low rate, so that it should not really press heavily

3. By extending it in the first instance only to real and funded property, mortgages &c, so as to exempt capitalists and professional persons from its effects, and to spare them the pains of exposure upon which so much

stress has been laid

The income tax produced in 1815 about £15,300,000, of which profits under schedule D yielded about £3,146,000, and occupiers under schedule B £2,176,000,[6] leaving about 10 million as the return from the species of property which it is now proposed to subject to contribution, this return must have then represented an income of at least 100 millions, and a capital exceeding 2,000 millions. There can be no doubt but that since that time, the public wealth has enormously increased so as far more than to compensate for the depreciation of the currency which then occurred. If we were to reckon the property now existing at 3,000 millions, we should probably not exaggerate its value, notwithstanding the fall in land, especially as Ireland was exempted from the income tax but ought of course it present to be exposed to the same burdens as the rest of the empire. However it must be recollected that the schedule E on salaries, would now produce less than during the war, and in order to avoid of exaggerating, the existing taxable property, other than commercial capitals, may be taken at 2,500 million, which is doubtless greatly within the truth. 2s per cent on the above sum would furnish $2\frac{1}{2}$ millions per annum.

It is obvious that a property tax thus constituted would be grossly unequal, as traders and professional men would be altogether free from it. The best practical mode of reaching them would be to establish an impost somewhat resembling the Droit des Patentes in France. They should be divided into classes and each individual in every class should be required to pay annually a certain fixed sum. It is impossible in the present work to give in detail a plan for effecting the object in view: but there seems no doubt, but that a little ingenuity would obviate all overwhelming objections to it. That it would be perfectly equal nobody can pretend; still this inconvenience must

---

[6] See Marshall's Tables p. 27. [Marshall, op. cit., Part II, p. 27 gives the Nett Schedule D figure for 1815 as £3,146,382 and the Nett Schedule B figure as £2,176,228 out of a total of £15,298,983.]

Possible Reduction of Expenditure	£2,000,000
House Tax	£1,200,000
Timber Duty	£300,000
Property Tax	£2,500,000
Tax on Trades and Professions	£1,500,000
	£9,500,000

be submitted to, if as it appears the unpopularity of an inquisition under certain circumstances, into the private concerns of individuals in trade is invincible. By the above tax, it is proposed to levy £1,540,000 per annum.

Let us now recapitulate the results obtained in the several items we have examined.

It now therefore remains to be seen how this large sum may be best employed in replacing, and thus providing for the abolition of the most pernicious existing imposts.

There can be no hesitation in selecting for removal in the first place the most objectionable of the corruptive and unequal taxes examined in chapters 9, 10 and 11, and one or two others producing similar effects, to which the reader is referred for a full explanation of their pernicious effects.[7]

The next class of taxes which it might be expedient to diminish and modify though not at present wholly to remove, are those on consumption. They are pernicious in themselves, and their reduction as affording an immediate increase to the comforts of the great mass of the population would in some degree tend to popularize the whole scheme, and thus yield support [for] those parts of it, which are founded on principles of utility obvious to untutored eyes.

---

[7][The figures provided by Norman are broadly correct, with the exception of the figure for the Post Office where he has slipped by £100,000. Marshall, op. cit., pp. 15, 17, 19 provides the following figures: Stamps on deeds, law proceedings, &c. £1,412,553; Marine insurance £222,824; Fire insurance £799,353; Newspapers £554,789; Advertisements £156,899; Stage coaches £422,543; Excise on paper £702,739; Duty on auctions £219,826; Duty on post horses £231,863; Post Office Great Britain £1,391,006; Post Office Ireland £139,200; Post Office £1,530,206; Stamps on bills of exchange £469,076; Receipts £215,739; Total £6,938,410.]

Stamp Duties on Deeds and Law Proceedings	£1,412,000
Duties on Marine Insurances	£220,000
Duty on Fire Insurances (1831)	(£799,000)
Duty on Fire Insurances	£750,000
Stamps on Newspapers	£554,000
Duty on Advertisements	£150,000
Duty on Stage Coaches	£422,000
Excise on Paper	£702,000
Duty on Auctions	£219,000
Duty on Post Horses	£231,000
Post Office Revenue	£1,430,000
Stamps on Bills of Exchange	£469,000
Duty on Receipts	£215,000
	£6,780,000

The most important articles in general use, whose price is now preposterously raised by a heavy taxation are sugar and tea. The use of both is conducive to health and good morals, and many advantages would result from diminishing their price. Such a reduction should be made in the tax on each, as to lower the revenue to the extent of £100,000, taking as a basis the average importation of the last few years. This would allow about 25 per cent to be taken off from the impost on sugar, while at the same time the drawback should be proportionably diminished and so arranged as no longer to act as a burden on the people of England to the extent of another million per annum. The impost on East and West Indian sugar should be equalized. The duty on tea would be diminished in the proposed scheme to the extent of about 30 per cent.

The excise on malt and glass is eminently interferent from the mode in which it is levied. It prevents in the preparation of these commodities the adoption of the best and cheapest processes, and of course deteriorates their qualities, and thus costs to the consumer much more than the gain to the exchequer. Yet as these taxes, especially the former are not necessarily more exceptionable, than many others that would remain after their abolition, it would be merely requisite to remodel them, so as to remove the obstruction their mode of collection now opposes to the skill of the producer. Some sacrifice on the part of the Exchequer might be requisite to attain this object effectually, and for that half a million may be allowed.

The first catalogue of Taxes	
Proposed for abolition amounted to	£6,780,000
Added to these are those on Tea	£1,000,000
Sugar	£1,000,000
Malt and Glass	£500,000
	£9,280,000

The above sum would leave a considerable balance which might be employed in diminishing or removing the taxes on small articles which produce little and are prodigal in collection. It is unnecessary to particularize them.

It might be confidently anticipated that the financial scheme now recommended, would, if adopted, be followed by a large increase in the produce of the taxes still remaining. This increase might be safely calculated at a million per annum; it would probably far exceed that sum. The surplus thus accruing should be employed in replacing the most pernicious of the remaining taxes which should be contemporaneously abolished.

The excise on bricks, tiles, and hops, and the customs on timber and many other articles might be diminished, and along with them a large deduction should be made as soon as circumstances allowed from the present extravagant imposts on spirits and tobacco. Enough has been already said to shew the injustice which generally accompanies heavy taxation, on what are called luxuries, and arguments have been offered tending to prove that morality is seldom promoted by fiscal measures, or at any rate that if some good arises from them in this point of view, it is accompanied by a more than countervailing amount of evil, or at any rate that the good might be attained more safely and certainly by direct legislation.[8] But however this may be, it cannot be denied that taxes should never be raised so high as to hold out an irresistible temptation to the smuggler, as is the case with those on spirits and tobacco. They should therefore as speedily as possible be reduced so low, that ordinary precaution on the part of the public authorities might suffice to protect the revenue from fraud. One immediate consequence of this plan, would be a saving of the enormous expenditure now incurred for the coast guard &c &c, which exceeds half a million yearly, this sum being thus left available for the diminution or removal of other impolitic imposts.

A great change in the public mind with respect to taxation would probably take place within a short period after the proposed scheme had come into operation. Almost every body would find that his income went farther than before, that he was practically richer in a much greater degree than could be accounted for by the naked diminution in the national expenditure. The well being of the community would advance with accelerated speed, and direct imposts become less unpopular than now. Immediate advantage should be taken of this alteration in the popular voice, by increasing the property tax as fast as circumstances might allow, and lessening or altogether abolishing the indirect taxes that might still remain; and when all the latter had been thus commuted, the direct imposts, with the exception of the land tax might also be removed, leaving the latter and the property tax to supply all the wants of the Government, as proposed in the chapter 32.

It is hardly necessary to mention that the corn-laws and every other legislative enactment, tending to benefit sellers at the expense of buyers, should be erased from the statute book. Almost the only monopoly which it would be wise to retain would be that of the currency, which it can be clearly shewn ought always to remain in the hands of the Government, or of

---

[8]See Sir H P on Fin Refm p. 45 et seq. [Parnell, op. cit., chapter iv, 'Taxes on Luxuries' pp. 38-59. Page 45 gives examples of increases in revenue following reductions in the duties on tea, coffee and spirits.]

some body acting under its control, and possessing a special delegation from it. Anything more on this head would be foreign to the object of this work.

It may be once more remarked in conclusion that most of the evils resulting from the National Debt would cease with the abolition of the impolitic taxes now employed to pay the interest, excepting the very small sum really necessary to defray the expense of collection; and this evil might perhaps be balanced by the convenience which the public funds afford to borrowers and lenders; in other words to the sellers and purchasers of annuities and obligations granted by the State. Were these at once paid off, a considerable period would elapse before private ingenuity had devised any plan, which could attain the same end equally well, if at all. It is hardly necessary to call to the reader's attention that it matters not so far as regards the national wealth, whether any given sum of income say £1,000, belongs wholly to A, we will suppose a landowner or whether he pays £200 in a tax which is subsequently disbursed in liquidation of a perpetual annuity to B, a fundholder. The real evil in the case was the abstraction from the national capital, which took place when the loan was contracted which the annuity now represents. The amount borrowed was altogether destroyed for an object, probably useless, possibly pernicious.

Should it however be thought expedient to diminish or altogether pay off the National Debt, our scheme of finance would afford facilities for the operation superior to any other, and would render it easy and simple in point of principle, and difficult only from its magnitude.

The same line of argument which shows that but little mischief would arise from the National Debt was the interest derived from a strictly scientific taxation, would also seem to show that future loans might when required be contracted without any serious inconvenience. But the cases are not precisely similar; the power of borrowing necessarily leads to extravagance on the part of the Government, and should never therefore be granted except in the event of an overwhelming necessity. Much more might be said on this subject, but it hardly falls within the object of this work, which has been already perhaps extended beyond due bounds. On this account chiefly the present chapter has been confined to little more than a mere sketch, which to do justice to it, would require numerous and important developments. Literal accuracy in figures has not been aimed at.

Index

ability to pay xvii, xviii–xix, xxi
accumulation, tax on 56
ad valorem duties 28–9, 67, 87, 94, 99, 105, 190
advantages of taxation 7–12
advertisements 124, 132, 192, 193
alcohol, taxes on *see* barley tax; beer tax; champagne tax; gin tax; hops tax; malt tax; spirits tax; wine tax
annuitants
  capitalisation of incomes of 178–9
  taxes falling on 93, 97, 152–3, 155
armorial bearings, tax on 113
assessed taxes, types of 113, 159–60
attorneys, fees on enrolment of 112, 123
auctions, duty on 192, 193

balance of trade 90, 104
Bank of England 24
bankruptcy 174, 175
Barbary 125
barley tax 102, 106
barter 89
beer tax 101
benefit principle xxi
Bengal 148
Bentham, J. xvi, xxxi–xxxii
bills of exchange, duty on xxxvii, 124, 192, 193
bonds 24, 70
books, taxes on *see* knowledge, taxes on
bounties 50–51, 77, 103
bricks, duty on 194
bridge tolls *see* turnpike and bridge tolls
building speculation 144–6
Burlington House 160
Byskat (Town Tax) 180

Cairnes, John Elliot xv

canals, provision of 10
Cannan, E. 2, 149
Canton 108
capital levy xxxvi, 70
capitalists, taxes falling on 93, 97, 105, 152–3, 155, 171–2
cards and dice, tax on 124
  see also gambling houses, tax on
carriages, tax on 113, 115, 159
certainty xvii
champagne tax 95
China 18, 108
Cholesbury, Buckinghamshire 146
churches, maintenance of 11
cigars, duty on 95
circulating property 24–5
civilisation, travelling and letter-writing as indicator of 120
Classical economics xxvi–xxvii, xl
coal, export duty on 91
coast guard 195
coastal blockade 98
Code of Commerce, French 180
coffee, duty on 90, 195
Cohen-Stuart, A.J. xxi
collection costs *see* frugality in collection
colonies 84, 90, 186–7
commercial capital xxxv–xxxvi, 24–5
commodity taxes, qualities of 22–3, 28–9, 67, 70
common rate of profit 49, 78, 87, 136, 139
competitively produced items, taxes on xxvi
compliance costs xix, xxxi
computability xx, 21–6, 39–40
  customs duties and xxviii, 98
  definition 21
  direct taxes on luxuries and xxviii, 114

excise taxes and xxviii, 102
health taxes and xxviii, 130
income tax and xxviii, 172
ingenuity taxes and xxviii, 130
insurance taxes and xxviii, 130
justice taxes and xxviii
knowledge taxes and xxviii, 130
legacy duty and xxviii, 155
modus and xxviii
partial taxes and xxviii, 110
poll tax and xxviii, 152
poor rate and xxviii, 146
postal taxes and 118
probate duty and xxviii, 155
property transfer taxes and xxviii, 130
single property tax and xxviii, xxxvi,
    182
taxes classified by xxviii
tithes and xxviii, 140
travelling taxes and xxviii, 118
vice taxes and xxviii, 168
constancy xx, 37–8, 40
  customs duties and 98
  definition 37
  direct taxes on luxuries and xxviii,
    114
  excise taxes and xxviii, 103
  health taxes and xxviii, 130
  income tax and 172
  ingenuity taxes and xxviii, 130
  insurance taxes and xxviii, 130
  justice taxes and xxviii, 124
  knowledge taxes and xxviii, 130
  legacy duty and xxviii, 155
  modus and xxviii
  partial taxes and xxviii, 110
  poll tax and xxviii, 152
  poor rate and xxviii, 146
  postal taxes and 118
  probate duty and xxviii, 155
  property transfer taxes and xxviii, 130
  single property tax and xxviii, 183
  taxes classified by xxviii
  tithes and xxviii, 140
  travelling taxes and xxviii, 118
  vice taxes and xxviii, 168
contributors, number of 33
convenience of payment xvii, xxiv, 161
conveyancing 133
conveyance of intelligence, taxes on *see*
    postal taxes
Corn Laws 86, 102, 106, 185, 195
corn rent xxxiii, 141–2
Cornwallis, Lord Charles 148

cotton, export duty on 91
countervailing duties 91
country and parish assessments 163
Court of Requests 126
Courts of Justice, fees paid in 123, 124,
    127
Crawford, John 95
currency
  changes in value of 89
  government monopoly of 195–6
customs duties 93–9
  collection costs 32–3, 98
  definition 84
  incidence of 93–4
  motives for 85
  proposals for reform xxxvii, 189–90,
    192, 193, 194
  qualities of xx, xxiii–xxiv, xxviii, xxix,
    xxx–xxxi, 61, 62, 85–91, 93–9
  revenue from 98
  types of 85, 93
  see also export duties; import duties

Daunton, M. xxxi
deadweight loss, conventional xxv, xxvi
debts 24–5
deeds, stamp duties on 192, 193
demoralisation 47, 80
Denmark, property registration in 179
despotic governments 34–5
Dickens, Charles xxxii
differentiation xxxv, xxxix
direct taxes
  abolition of 195
  definition 83, 113
  versus indirect taxes xvi, xxiv
  see also health taxes; house tax;
      income tax; ingenuity, taxes on;
      insurance taxes; justice, taxes on;
      knowledge, taxes on; land tax;
      legacy duty; luxuries, taxes on;
      newspapers; poll tax; poor rate;
      postal taxes; probates of wills,
      stamp duty on; property taxes;
      property transfer taxes; rent
      taxes; tithes; travelling, taxes on;
      turnpike and bridge tolls; vice
      taxes; window tax
divisibility xx, 39–41
  customs duties and 98
  definition 39
  direct taxes on luxuries and xxviii,
    114
  excise taxes and xxviii, 103

health taxes and xxviii, 130
income tax and xxviii, 172
ingenuity taxes and xxviii, 130
insurance taxes and xxviii, 130
justice taxes and xxviii, 124
knowledge taxes and xxviii, 130
legacy duty and xxviii, 155
modus and xxviii
partial taxes and xxviii, 110
poll tax and xxviii, 152
poor rate and xxviii, 146
postal taxes and 118
probate duty and xxviii, 155
property transfer taxes and xxviii, 130
single property tax and xxviii, xxxvi, 183
taxes classified by xxviii
tithes and xxviii, 140
travelling taxes and xxviii, 118
vice taxes and xxviii, 168
division of labour 7–9
drawbacks 51–2
Droit des Patentes 112, 191
Droits réunis 69, 106
drunkenness 79–81

earnings, taxes on xxxv
East India Company 70, 107–8
economic growth xvii, xxi, xxxix
economical effects of taxation xxv, 17
economy in collection xviii
    see also frugality in collection
Edinburgh Review 86
education services 10–11
elasticity of supply xxvi, xxx
employers, poll tax assessed on 153–4
employment
    effect of servants tax on 115
    see also public employees
England
    assessed taxes in 66
    corruptive taxes in 62
    customs and excise taxes in 32–3, 95, 98, 101, 105
    income tax in xxiv, 171–5
    inconveniences of tax payment in 66
    land tax in 142
    least evasible taxes in 69–70
    partial taxes in 109–12
    postal taxes in 117
    property registration in 179
    stamp duty on probates and letter of administration in 156
    tax officials employed in 32–3

tithes in 135–6
    see also Great Britain; United Kingdom
equality xvii, xx, 53–8
    customs duties and xxix, 99
    definition 53
    differentiation necessary for xxxv
    direct taxes on luxuries and xxix, 115
    excise taxes and xxix, 105
    income tax and xxix, 173–4
    insurance taxes and 132
    land tax and 142
    justice taxes and xxix, 125–6
    knowledge taxes and 132
    legacy duty and xxix, 156–7, 188
    moral equality xix
    multiple taxes necessary for xxxviii
    partial taxes and 111
    poll tax and 152–3
    poor rate and xxix, 147
    postal taxes and 117, 119
    probate duty and xxix, 156
    property transfer tax and 131–2
    proportionality and xxi–xxiii, 53–8, 99, 115, 119, 126, 157, 173, 183
    single property tax and 183
    stamp duties generally and 161
    Taille and 149
    taxes classified by xxix
    tithes and 141
    travelling taxes and xxix, 117, 119, 164–5
    vice taxes and xxix, 168
Europe
    excise taxes in 104, 106–7
    spirits taxes in 80
    see also under individual European countries e.g. France; Italy
excess revenues 37–8
excise taxes 101–8
    collection costs 32–3, 103
    definition 84, 101
    incidence of 102
    motives for xxx, 102
    proposals for reform xxxvii, 193–5
    qualities of xxviii, xxix, xxx–xxxi, 61, 62, 66, 102–8, 185
    revenue from 103, 192, 193
export duties xxx, 19, 76, 89, 90–91

farmers, tax paid by 171–2, 174, 181
farming of taxes 34–5, 118
fashion 48
fees of office 109

fees paid in Courts of Justice 123, 124, 127
Fermiers generaux 34
financial circumstances of taxpayer, publication of 66
fire insurance 132, 192, 193
fixed incomes, direct tax on 94, 95
fixed property 23–4, 143
forts 10
France
    corruptive taxes in 62
    cost of roads in 165–6
    evasible taxes in 69–70
    excise taxes in 104, 106–7
    farming of taxes in 34
    fees levied by corporations in 112, 191
    property registration in 179–80
    rent taxes in 148–9
    tax collection cost in 31
free trade 107, 142
French Code of Commerce 180
French fire offices 131
French Revolution 149
frugality in collection xx, 31–5
    customs duties and 98
    direct taxes on luxuries and xxviii, 114
    excise taxes and 103, 107
    health taxes and xxviii, 130
    income tax and xxviii, 172
    ingenuity taxes and xxviii, 130
    insurance taxes and xxviii, 130
    justice taxes and xxviii, 124
    knowledge taxes and xxviii, 130
    legacy duty and xxviii, 124, 155
    Norman's definition xix, 31
    partial taxes and 110
    poll tax and xxviii, 152
    poor rate and xxviii, 146
    popularity and 42
    postal taxes and 118
    probate duty and xxviii, 155
    property transfer taxes and xxviii, 130
    single property tax and xxviii, xxxvi, 183
    Smith's definition xviii
    taxes classified by xxviii
    tithes and xxviii, 140
    travelling taxes and xxviii, 118, 164
    uncorruptiveness and 60
    vice taxes and 167–8

Gabelle 107
gambling houses, tax on xxxiv, 61, 124, 167–9

game duty 113
gifts 188
Gilbert, P. 180
Gilbert, W.S. xxxii
gin tax 95
glass tax xxxvii, 50, 105, 193–4
government expenditure
    increase in xxxvii, xxxix–xl
    minimisation of xviii, xxvii, xxxvi, 11, 76, 186–7, 192
government officials
    frequent presence and inspection of 66, 116, 175
    powers of 65
Great Britain
    advertisements in 132
    customs and excise taxes in 103–4
    justice taxes in 124–5
    legacy duty in 124
    postal taxes in 117–18, 192, 193
    road cost in 165
    spirits taxes in 80
    state lotteries in 167–8
    total tax collection costs in 32, 103
    total tax receipts in 32
    see also England; Scotland; United Kingdom
Greece 54
Grote, George xvi, xix, xxii–xxiii, xxxii, 54, 120, 140
ground rent 144–6
gunpowder 102

hackney carriages, taxes on 110, 117
hackney coach board 118
hair powder, tax on 113, 159
Hamburg 42–3, 67
harbours, provision of 10
Hastings xxiv, 61
hawkers and pedlars, taxes on 110, 117
health, taxes on 161
    motivation for 129
    qualities of xxviii, xxix, 129, 130
Higgs, E. 184
honours, rewarding by xviii, 11
hops tax 101, 102, 194
horses, tax on 113, 115
    see also post horses, tax on
hospitals 11
Houghton, E.R. 95
Houghton, W.E. 95
house tax 84
    incidence of xxvii, 146, 159, 188–9
    on mansions xxxiii, 160

proposals for reform xxxvi, 160, 188–9, 192
qualities of 70, 146, 185
Hubbard, J.G. xxxv

import duties
  adverse consequences of xxv–xxvi, xxvii, 46–50, 85–90, 93–9
  corruptiveness of 60–61
  proposals for reform 189–90, 192, 193, 194
  simplicity of 28–9
impôt foncier 148–9
income tax 171–5
  abolition of xxxiv–xxxv, 171, 173, 175
  collection costs of 172
  incidence of 171–2
  Norman's enthusiasm for xxxiv–xxxv
  as part of a general system of taxation xxxviii–xxxix
  qualities of xxiv, xxviii, xxix, 70, 172–5
  revenue from xxx, 172, 191
  scales in England 173–4
income tax records xxxiv–xxxv
India, rent taxes in 147–8
indirect taxes 83–91
  abolition of 195
  definition 83
  evil occasioned by 85–91
  interference of 51
  motives for establishing 85
  popularity of 67, 96
  types of 83–5
  unevasibility of 69
  versus direct taxes xvi, xxiv
infrastructure provision 10
ingenuity, taxes on 161
  incidence of 130
  motive for 129
  qualities of xxviii, xxix, 129, 130, 131
inheritance tax *see* legacy duty
insolvent traders, income tax paid by 174, 175
insufficient revenues 37
insurance taxes
  abolition of xxxvii
  incidence of 130, 161
  motive for 129
  qualities of xxviii, xxix, xxxii, 129, 130, 131, 132
  revenue from 192, 193
intoxication 79–81

Ireland
  exempt from income tax 191
  postal taxes in 117–18, 192, 193
  total tax collection costs in 32
  total tax receipts in 32
Italy
  excise taxes in 106–7
  farming of taxes in 34–5
  insecurity of property in 125

Jamaica 90
Jews, taxes paid by 66
juries 181
justice, taxes on 123–8
  abolition of xxxvii
  collection costs 124
  definition 123
  incidence of 124
  motive for 124
  qualities of xxviii, xxix, xxxi–xxxii, 66, 112, 124–8
  revenues from 124, 192, 193
  types of 123, 160

knowledge, taxes on
  incidence of 161
  motive for 129–30
  qualities of xxviii, xxix, 129, 130, 131
  see also newspapers

labour theory of value xxii
land, equal distribution of 54
land revenue 147–8
land surveys 148–9
land tax
  proposals for reform 188, 195
  qualities of xxxiii, 70, 142
landlords, taxes falling on 93, 97, 105, 152–3, 171–2
law taxes *see* justice, taxes on
leather tax 102
legacy duty
  collection costs 124, 155
  incidence of 155, 184, 187
  proposals for reform 157–8, 187–8
  qualities of xxviii, xxix, 155–7
  on real property xxxii, 156, 187
  revenues from 12, 187
letters and parcels, tax on conveyancing of *see* postal taxes
letters of administration, stamp duty on 155, 156–7
licences 84
London, building speculation in 145, 146

lotteries 61, 167–9
Lotteries Act (1823) 167
luxuries, taxes on 81–2
    direct taxes 113–16
        examples of 113, 159
        incidence of 114
        motive for 113–14
        qualities of xxviii, xxix, 114–16
    indirect taxes 85, 93, 95–6
Lycurgus 54

machinery to labour ratio 153
malt tax xxxvii, 50, 69, 101, 102, 104,
    105, 106, 193–4
mansions, tax on xxxiii, 160
manure, toll-free carrying of 165
marine insurances, taxes on 131, 192,
    193
Marshall, J. 31–2, 98, 103, 114, 117–18,
    124, 156, 167–8, 172, 187, 189, 191,
    192
McCulloch, J.R. xvii, xxi, xxiii, xxiv, 2–3,
    56, 86, 118, 124, 156, 184, 189
mercantile letters and parcels 117
mercantile stamps 84
Mill, James xvi, xxxii
Mill, John Stuart xvi, xix, xxi, xxiii
minimum sacrifice, criteria for xix–xxiv
modus xxviii, xxix, 135
money
    sacrifice of, to discharge tax
        obligations 66
    tax paid in form of 18
'monopolised' articles, taxes on xxvi,
    xxx, 84, 89–90
    excise tax 102, 106
moral effects of taxation xxv, 2–3, 17
moral equality xix
mortgages 24, 70
motives for taxation 75–82
munitions, duties on 76
murderers, tax on 61

Napoleonic wars xxxiv
National Debt 182, 196
national defence xxvii, 76
national security 78
national wealth, taxes to increase 76,
    77–8
navigation laws 76, 78
necessaries, taxes on xxvi–xxvii, 58, 85,
    93, 94–5, 105
newspapers
    conveyed free of expense 121

stamp duty on xxxii, xxxvii, 129–30,
    161, 192, 193
non-tax revenues 18–20
noninterference xx–xxi, 45–52
    customs duties and xxix, 99, 104
    definition 45
    direct taxes on luxuries and xxix, 115
    excise taxes and xxix, 104–5
    health taxes and xxix
    income tax and xxix, 173
    ingenuity taxes and xxix, 130, 131
    insurance taxes and xxix, 130, 131
    justice taxes and xxix, 125–6
    knowledge taxes and xxix, 130, 131
    legacy duty and xxix, 155
    partial taxes and xxix, 111
    poll tax and xxix, 152
    poor rate and xxix, 146
    postal taxes and 119
    probate duty and xxix, 155
    property transfer taxes and xxix,
        130–31
    single property tax and xxix, xxxvi,
        183
    taxes classified by xxix
    tithes and xxix, 140
    travelling taxes and xxix, 119, 164
    uncorruptiveness and 60
    vice taxes and xxix, 168
Norman, G.W. xv, xxi
Northcote, H.S. xxxviii
Norway
    Norman's trips to 87
    property registration in 179, 180

O'Brien, D.P. xv, xix, xx, xxii, xxiii, xxiv,
    xxvi, xxvii, xxxiii, xxxiv, xxxv,
    xxxvi, xxxviii, 2, 3, 56, 156
oaths, violation of 60, 61, 62, 99
opium 102, 107–8
Overstone, Lord (Samuel Jones Loyd)
    xx, xxx, xxxviii

paper, excise on 192, 193
parliamentary grants 163
Parnell, Henry 3, 23, 31, 51, 93–4, 110,
    117, 132, 195
partial taxes 109–12
    incidence of 109–10, 159–60
    motives for 109
    for public employees 8
    qualities of xxviii, xxix, xxxi, 110–12
particular classes and persons, taxes on
    see partial taxes

pawnbrokers 111
payment in kind 18
  see also tithes
pecuniary circumstances of taxpayer,
  publication of 66
Peel, Sir Robert xxxvii–xxxviii, xxxix
penalties
  for intoxication 81
  taxes as 120–21
Penny Post 118
pensions 103, 118
permanent incomes, taxes on xxxv,
  xxxix
permanent settlement 148
petitions 130
Peto, Samuel Morton xxxviii
placemen, taxing of 182
places of worship, toll-free travelling to
  165
planks, duty on 86–7
Plutarch 54
political economy and taxation 1–5
Political Economy Club 2, 184
political power, taxes to increase 76,
  78–9
poll tax 151–4
  incidence of 151–2
  proposals for reform 153–4
  qualities of xxviii, xxix, xxxiii–xxxiv,
    28, 152–3
Poor Law Amendment Bill 147
poor rate xxxiii, 11
  books of 24
  incidence of xxvii, 143–6
  qualities of xxviii, xxix, 146–7
popularity xx, 41–3
  customs duties and xxviii, xxx–xxxi,
    96, 99
  definition 41
  direct taxes on luxuries and xxviii,
    114–15
  and evasibility 42–3, 70, 97, 103–4
  excise taxes and xxviii, xxx–xxxi,
    103–4, 185
  health taxes and xxviii, 130
  income tax and xxviii, 173
  of indirect taxes generally 67, 96
  ingenuity taxes and xxviii, 130
  insurance taxes and xxviii, 130
  justice taxes and 124
  knowledge taxes and xxviii, 130
  legacy duty and xxviii, 155
  modus and xxviii
  partial taxes and 110–11

poll tax and 152
poor rate and xxviii, 146–7
postal taxes and 118–19
probate duty and xxviii, 155
property transfer taxes and xxviii, 130
single property tax and 183, 184, 185
stamp duties generally and 161, 185
taxes classified by xxviii
tithes and xxviii, 139–40
travelling taxes and xxviii, 118–19,
  164
vice taxes and xxviii, 168
population census 28
post horses, tax on 117, 124, 192, 193
Post Office 117–18, 192
postal taxes 10, 117–21
  motive for 117
  qualities of 117–21
  revenue from 117–18, 192, 193
precious metals, import and export of
  85, 89
Prinsep, C.R. 16
prisons 10, 47, 107
probates of wills, stamp duty on
  incidence of 155
  proposals for reform 157–8, 187
  qualities of xxviii, xxix, 155–6
  on real property xxxii, 156, 187
  revenues from 124, 187
  scale in England 156
production costs 88, 104–5
productiveness xx, 71
professional capital xxxvi, 24–5
professions, taxes on *see* trades and
  professions, taxes on
profits taxes xxxv, 61, 70, 159, 171–2,
  191
progressive taxation xxi, xxiii, 56–7, 183
prohibitions 50, 77
property registration xxxv, 23–6, 70,
  133, 178–82
property taxes
  introduction of 'very light' xxxvii,
    190–91, 192
  qualities of xxiv, 23–6, 29, 66, 67, 70
  revenue raising capacity of xxx
  single improved property tax xxxiv,
    177–84, 195
    capitalisation of annuities 178–9
    exemptions from xxxv, xxxvi, 178,
      182
    fiscal districts 179
    payment periods 181
    proportionality of xxxv, 178, 183

publication of property lists 178
qualities of xxviii, xxix, xxxv–xxxvi,
   182–4, 185
registration of property necessary
   for xxxv, 178, 179–82
as tax on capital 157
types of xxxiii
   see also house tax; land tax; poor
      rate; rent taxes; tithes; window
      tax
property transfer taxes
   incidence of 130, 160–61
   motive for 129
   qualities of xxviii, xxix, xxxii, 129,
      130–32, 133
proportionality
   and equality xxi–xxiii, 53–8, 99, 115,
      119, 126, 157, 173, 183
   of single property tax xxxv, 178, 183
prudence, taxes on 56
   see also insurance taxes
public debt 70
public employees
   number of xviii, 11, 32–3
   remuneration of xviii, xix, 8–10, 11
public enlightenment 41, 81
public expenditure
   increase in xxxvii, xxxix–xl
   minimisation of xviii, xxvii, xxxvi, 11,
      76, 186–7, 192

quarantine expenses 98

raw materials, taxes on 84, 85, 90, 93–5
real property
   legacy duty and probate duty on xxxii,
      156, 187
   property tax on 179, 190
receipts, duty on 124, 192, 193
Reform Act (1832) xxiii
registration of property xxxv, 23–6, 70,
   133, 178–82
regressive taxation xxiii
religious belief xxxii
rent
   increasing with population and wealth
      136–7
   meaning of 136
rent taxes xxvii, xxxiii, 19, 61, 94, 95,
   159
   in India 147–8
   in France 148–9
   see also house tax; income tax; land
      tax; poor rate; tithes; window tax

reputation 70
resource misallocation loss xxv, xxvi
return for capital embarked 144–6
revenue raising capacity xxx, 16, 22–3,
   26, 29, 71, 114
Ricardo, D. xxii, xxxiii, xxxvi, 2, 3, 19,
   115, 184
roads
   provision of 10, 165–6
   see also turnpike and bridge tolls
Romans, taxes paid to 66
Russia 151
ryots 148

salaries and allowances, expenditure on
   103, 118
   see also public employees
salt tax 33, 102, 107
Say, J.B. 2, 3, 15–16
schedule A income tax 172
schedule B income tax 191
schedule D income tax 191
schedule E income tax 191
Scotland, postal taxes in 117
security
   to cultivators 148
   justice taxes opposed to 127
   national 78
Select Committee on Public Documents
   (1833) 32
servants, tax on 113, 115, 159
shipping, taxes on 163
simplicity xx, 27–30
   customs duties and xxviii, 98
   definition 27
   direct taxes on luxuries and xxviii, 114
   excise taxes and 103
   health taxes and xxviii, 130
   income tax and xxviii, 172
   ingenuity taxes and xxviii, 130
   insurance taxes and xxviii, 130
   justice taxes and xxviii, 124
   knowledge taxes and xxviii, 130
   modus and xxviii
   partial taxes and 110
   poll tax and xxviii, 152
   poor rate and xxviii, 146
   postal taxes and 118
   property transfer taxes and xxviii, 130
   single property tax and 182–3
   taxes classified by xxviii
   travelling taxes and xxviii, xxxi, 118,
      164
   vice taxes and xxviii, 168

single property tax *see under* property
taxes
Sismondi, J.Simonde de 34–5
size, customs duties related to 86–7
Smith, Adam xxxii, 1–2, 8, 131–2, 149
canons of taxation xvii–xviii, 2
Spain
excise taxes in 106
farming of taxes in 34
insecurity of property in 125
Sparta 54
speculation 38, 46, 144–6, 172
Speenhamland system 147
spirits tax 63, 79–81, 101, 104, 105, 194,
195
Sraffa, P. 19, 115, 184
stage coaches, taxes on 117, 192, 193
stamp duties
qualities of xxviii, xxix, xxxii, 161, 185
types of xxxii, 160–61
see also bills of exchange, duty on;
deeds, stamp duties on; health,
taxes on; ingenuity, taxes on;
insurance taxes; knowledge, taxes
on; letters of administration,
stamp duty on; newspapers;
probates of wills, stamp duty on;
property transfer taxes; suits at
law, stamp duty on
Stark, W. xvi
state-owned monopolies 101–2, 106–7
state-owned property 19
Steintrager, J. xxxii
Storch, H.F. v. 2
subsistence minimum, exempt from
taxation xxii–xxiii, xxxv, 57, 174,
178
sugar tax xxxvii, 90, 96, 193, 194
suits at law, stamp duty on 123, 124,
127, 160, 192, 193
sumptuary taxes xxvii, xxx
superannuation 103
surcharges 116
surplus revenues 37–8

Taille 149
tale (number), customs duties related to
99
tariffs *see* import duties
tastes, changes in 88
tax, definition of 18
tax collection costs *see* frugality in
collection

tax exemption
preferential xxxvi, 53, 56, 182, 189,
190–92
of a subsistence minimum xxii–xxiii,
xxxv, 57, 174, 178
tax incidence xxiv–xxvii
tax increases, capacity for 39–40
tax payers, computability with respect
to 22
tax reductions, capacity for 39–40
tax returns xxiv, 66, 70, 97, 114, 116
tea tax xxxvii, 70, 96, 193, 194, 195
teetotum 40
temporary incomes, taxes on xxxv, xxxix
Tiers Etat 149
tiles, duty on 194
timber duties xxxvii, 61, 78, 86–7,
189–90, 192, 194
time, sacrifice of 66
tithes
application of 140
commutation for corn rent xxxiii,
141–2
consequences of abolishing 106, 138,
140
in England 135–6
qualities of xxviii, xxix, 139–41
as tax on rent xxxiii, 136–9
tobacco taxes 95, 102, 106, 194, 195
trade licences 84
trades and professions, taxes on xxxvi,
109–12, 159–60, 174–5, 181–2, 183,
190–92
transport costs 91
transport taxes xxviii, xxix
see also travelling, taxes on; turnpike
and bridge tolls
travelling, taxes on 117–21
definition of 117
motive for 117
qualities of xxviii, xxix, xxxi, 117–21,
164–5
revenue from 117, 192, 193
versus general taxation xxxi, 165–6
see also turnpike and bridge tolls
tributes from foreign states 19
Turkey
insecurity of property in 125
poll tax in 151
property registration in 180–81
turnpike and bridge tolls 163–6
qualities of 118, 164–5
versus general taxation xxxi, 165–6

uncorruptiveness xx, 59–63
  customs duties and xxiii–xxiv, xxix,
    97–8, 99
  definition 59
  direct taxes on luxuries and xxix, 115
  excise taxes and xxix, 105, 107–8
  health taxes and xxix, 132
  income tax and xxix, 174–5
  ingenuity taxes and xxix, 132
  insurance taxes and xxix, 132
  justice taxes and xxix, 126–7
  knowledge taxes and xxix, 132
  legacy duty and 157, 187
  modus and xxix
  partial taxes and 111–12
  poll tax and 152
  poor rate and xxix, 147
  postal taxes and 117, 119–20
  property taxes and 157
    single property tax xxxvi, 183–4
  property transfer taxes and xxix, 133
  rules for 60, 97
  taxes classified by xxix
  tithes and xxix, 140–41
  travelling taxes and xxix, 117, 119–20,
    164
  vice taxes and xxix, 168–9
  window tax and xxix, 146
unevasibility xx, xxiv, 69–71
  customs duties and xxix, 97–8, 99
  definition 69
  direct taxes on luxuries and 116
  excise taxes and xxix, 103–4, 105,
    106–7
  frugality and 33
  health taxes and xxix, 130
  income tax and xxiv, 175
  ingenuity taxes and xxix, 130
  insurance taxes and xxix, 130
  justice taxes and 124
  knowledge taxes and xxix, 130
  legacy duty and xxix, 155
  partial taxes and 112
  poll tax and xxix, 152
  poor rate and xxix, 146
  popularity and 42–3, 70, 97, 103–4
  postal taxes and 121
  probate duty and xxix, 155
  property transfer taxes and xxix, 130
  simplicity and 29
  single property tax and 184
  taxes classified by xxix
  tithes and xxix, 141
  travelling taxes and 121

  unvexatiousness and 70
  vice taxes and xxix, 168
United Kingdom
  postal taxes in 118
  see also England; Great Britain;
    Ireland; Scotland
United States
  advertisements in 132
  customs duties in 99
  spirits taxes in 80
unvexatiousness xx, xxiv, 65–8
  customs duties and xxix, 99
  definition 65
  direct taxes on luxuries and xxix,
    115–16
  and evasibility 70
  excise taxes and xxix, 105–6
  health taxes and xxix, 130
  income tax and 175
  ingenuity taxes and xxix, 130
  insurance taxes and xxix, 130
  justice taxes and 127
  knowledge taxes and xxix, 130
  legacy duty and 155
  partial taxes and 112
  poll tax and xxix, 153
  poor rate and 146–7
  postal taxes and 121
  property transfer taxes and xxix, 130
  single property tax and 184
  taxes classified by xxix
  tithes and 141
  travelling taxes and xxix, 121, 164
  vice taxes and xxix, 168
Urquhart, D. 180
useful actions, taxes on performance of
  60, 62–3
Utilitarianism xvi, xix, xxi, xxii–xxiii,
  xxvii–xxx, xxxi, xxxii, xl

vice taxes
  qualities of xxviii, xxix, xxxiv, 61–2,
    167–9
  types of xxxiv, 167
'viceincentive' xix
'viceincentiveness' xix
voluntary taxes 42–3, 67

wage goods, taxes on xxvi–xxvii, 58, 85,
  93, 94–5, 105
wage taxes 41, 57–8
Warburton, Henry xxxv
warehousing expenses 98

weight, customs duties related to 86, 99
Westminster Review 95
William III 142
wills *see* probates of wills, stamp duty
    on

window tax xxviii, xxix, xxxi, xxxiii,
    xxxvi, 84, 113, 146, 159, 189
wine tax 84, 95

Zemindars 148